RUGBY

THE PIONEER YEARS

RUGBY

THE PIONEER YEARS

Alan Turley

HarperCollinsPublishers

Published with the assistance of a grant from
the New Zealand Rugby Foundation

National Library of New Zealand Cataloguing-in-Publication Data
Turley, Alan.
Rugby, the pioneer years / Alan Turley.
Includes bibliographical references and index.
ISBN 978-1-86950-684-1
1. Rugby Union football—New Zealand—History—19th century.
I. Title.
796.3330993—dc 22

First published 2008

HarperCollins*Publishers (New Zealand) Limited*
P.O. Box 1, Auckland

ISBN 978 1 86950 684 1

Cover design by Matt Stanton, HarperCollins Design Studio
Cover images: Team cap of the 1893 New Zealand team which
toured Australia (New Zealand Rugby Museum);
An unknown early New Zealand club team, circa 1885.
Inside cover: 'The College v Town'; artist Paul Wilding's
impression of the first match, 14 May 1870 (Nelson College).
Typesetting by Springfield West
Printed by Phoenix Offset, China, on 128 gsm Matt Art

*To those spirited
pioneering young men
who gave us rugby.*

The *New Zealand Graphic* of September 1892 entitled this engraving 'An up-country football match'.

Rugby Football is a game for muddied oafs.

Rudyard Kipling

Contents

Foreword

John Graham

Books on New Zealand rugby — the histories, the tours, the reminiscences, biographies, autobiographies and statistics — gather dust on the shelves of thousands of New Zealand rugby enthusiasts. Many of those books provide an easy annual choice for Christmas and birthday presents for dads, male relations and friends. Very few of this avalanche are insightful or even memorable. Yet this vast and varied library satisfies the remarkable appetite of New Zealand rugby followers for our national game, its triumphs, tribulations, personalities and villains.

However, no one has attempted to do what Alan Turley has done in *Rugby: The Pioneer Years*. His work fills a genuine and significant gap in our rugby union lore and history by providing for the first time, in one volume, a historical narrative of our national game prior to 1900.

His story starts in Roman times and journeys through the beginnings of the game in village mauls in England, its refinement at Rugby School in the early 19th century and its growth in other parts of Britain, then on to the introduction of aspects of the game in New Zealand in the 1860s. Alan Turley follows the fascinating development of our game through clubs, schools, provinces, national sides and tours to the beginning of the 20th century.

The story contains a wealth of information on the steady, positive growth of the game — the debate, disagreements, disputes, personalities — based on the author's careful research, his regard for history and the difference between fact and fiction, as well as his personal respect for our national game. We also learn more about William Webb Ellis. There is a considered debate about which club is able to claim to be the first rugby club in New Zealand and a lengthy argument over the rules and how the game should be played. Thankfully, because of strong and visionary leaders, we avoided the threat of soccer and Australian rules, and ensured rugby football would be our game.

Featured also are the personalities who set the standards for the future, the rapid expansion of clubs nationwide, the establishment of provincial boundaries and the disputes and healthy rivalries that quickly developed, the importance of schools in the growth of the game and the legacy gradually established by all involved in those formative years which had led to the game becoming our national sporting passion. It is a remarkable and interesting story, reflecting the pioneering qualities of our forebears and their search for competitive, physical activity and the social and family interaction that became a crucial part of the game. Rugby suited the needs of those early times and it has suited us ever since.

Throughout the narrative are 'panels' adding fascinating historical information on aspects of our game that does not fit naturally in to the narrative. There are close to a hundred illustrations, which add a special flavour.

I commend Alan Turley's *Rugby: The Pioneer Years* to all those who have a genuine interest in our game and a feeling for its history. Where debates and arguments occur over the early history of rugby football in New Zealand, this book provides many of the answers. As well, it is an authentic, historical record of the first thirty years. It fills the gap that has been waiting on the rugby enthusiasts' bookshelves.

D. John Graham CBE
President, the Rugby Foundation of New Zealand
Past President, New Zealand Rugby Football Union

Foreword

Sir Brian Lochore

IT IS A pleasure to write a foreword for this fascinating book, *Rugby: The Pioneer Years*. There has been an extraordinary amount of research gone into this publication. I applaud Alan Turley for having the foresight and enthusiasm to go into an area of rugby research that has not been covered before.

Anyone who enjoys rugby, and particularly rugby history, will not be able to put this book down once they have started reading it. The book, first of all, describes how rugby was developed as a game in England, how numbers participating in any one game varied enormously in the early matches. It covers the fact that initially there was no referee and no standardised rules, just rules decided by the two captains who controlled the match on the day. The book shows how the game grew and expanded from Rugby School to other areas of England and then onto Scotland, Ireland and Wales. I found this area, including how footballs were developed from pigs' bladders and leather, very fascinating. I thought I knew a little bit about the early development of rugby in New Zealand, but the detail and commentary of the progress of the game from a few British immigrants playing socially, to a way of getting men together away from work, through to forming clubs, playing competitions, then forming unions and on to administrators selecting provincial teams, adds greatly to this knowledge.

The book finishes at the end of the 19th century, before the time of the 1905 Originals. Many great photos are included. I recommend this book to you, not only as a great history of our great game, but also as a very good read.

Sir Brian Lochore
All Black Selector

Acknowledgements

No project such as this would be possible without the contributions of other people. I would like to express my thanks to John Graham, Past President of the New Zealand Rugby Football Union, who has been a driving force behind this project since its inception. His involvement and commitment together with contributions of information and material made it happen. John and Sir Brian Lochore have also provided valued foreword contributions, for which I am most grateful.

Noelene Ford has been a tower of strength and spent many hundreds of hours typing and correcting the text, and Sandra Birdling has handled the organisation of photographic material most willingly and capably.

During the course of my research I have leant on several rugby historians for assistance and they have been most helpful. In particular, Jed Smith, of the Museum of Rugby, Twickenham, and Bob Luxford, of the New Zealand Rugby Museum, went well beyond the call of duty in providing countless details of information and photographic material. David Ray (Rugby School), Jane Teal (Christ's College), Paddianne Neely (Wellington College) and Alan Trent (Christchurch Football Club) were also extremely obliging.

My thanks to Nelson College for use of the painting 'The College v Town', for the endpaper illustration.

My wife, Anne, has been understanding and most supportive while attending to all the secretarial responsibilities.

HarperCollins Publishers, in particular Managing Editor Eva Chan, have been a pleasure to work with at all times and have demonstrated professional expertise in designing and producing a first-class publication.

Finally, and most importantly, I owe a debt of gratitude to the New Zealand Rugby Foundation for providing the funding necessary to make this publication possible and to Rocky Patterson, Executive Officer of the foundation.

Introduction

My friend David Ray, master in charge of football at Rugby School in England, and an astute rugby historian, has referred to Rugby School as 'the birthplace of rugby in England' and to Nelson College as 'the cradle of rugby in New Zealand'. Of course, there were other significant contributors in both countries, but David's comment aptly reflects the part played by each school in the establishment of rugby in their respective country. Each was a major contributor and filled a crucial role.

On 1 August 1992, 150 years after William Webb Ellis is said to have made his celebrated dash with the ball, a significant event took place at Nelson College. Rugby School, while touring New Zealand, played Nelson College. The school that gave rugby to England and thence to the world, finally played Nelson College, the school that played the first game of rugby in New Zealand and was probably the first school outside Britain to play the game. In a sense, history had been fulfilled: the two celebrated schools finally met on the playing field.

In my capacity as a local councillor, I made a brief speech at the after-match function. I welcomed the Rugby School First XV, offered some laudatory comments about Rugby School and highlighted some historical aspects of the game. It was a poignant occasion and I enjoyed conversing with Rugby School staff about the development of the game at Rugby and its current status.

The occasion stirred my interest in the history of rugby and I began a cursory effort to research and write about the origins of rugby at Nelson College. However, there was a paucity of historical information in the college archives and I was obliged to search further afield. In the process I became engrossed in the whole phenomenon of early New Zealand rugby.

I soon discovered that there was no specific written record focusing on the beginnings of rugby in New Zealand. Although several people have written on particular aspects of early rugby or produced limited material, it has remained a largely untold story. It is a story that needs to be told, though, because no other activity has contributed so much to the New

Zealand way of life and to our sense of national identity as the game of rugby.

Now, having produced other material on early New Zealand rugby, I have finally committed to writing a full exposition on how we achieved our national game. The account begins in England, because that is where the story of New Zealand rugby begins. It concludes in New Zealand at about the turn of the 20th century, because it is from this point that other rugby historians have picked up the story and related it in comprehensive detail. It is my hope that this account will fill the gap in the recorded history of our national game and form an integral part of the overall story of rugby in New Zealand.

The written material on our pioneer rugby is scant and sometimes confusing. Our rugby forefathers never fully realised the great adventure on which they were embarking. Besides, they were rugby players, not writers. Even the newspapers of the time initially gave the game little attention. The whole saga occurred without any intent, design or acclaim.

On the subject of illustrations, the science of photography was in its infancy in the 19th century. Photographic technology was not capable of capturing motion, so subjects had to be stationary. The only other material available was artists' drawings or impressions of events, of which few were produced in New Zealand. I have tried not to bore the reader with a plethora of old rugby team photographs, of which there are plenty available, but rather to use selections that relate to topics within the text.

Over the years, the methods of scoring and the value of the points scored have been subject to continual change. Similarly, the rules have also been changed and modified. I have avoided focusing on these aspects in too much detail, in order to avoid difficulties and confusion for the reader.

Finally, I pay tribute to those pioneering young men, who took this game by the neck, nurtured it, helped it grow and bequeathed it to future generations. Although now largely forgotten, men like Charles Monro, Robert Tennant, Alfred Drew, Croasdaile Bowen, Robert Harman, Thomas Henderson, George Thomson, Montague Lewin, Alfred St George Hamersley, William Millton, Joseph Firth, Edward Hoben, Samuel Sleigh and Tom Ellison must never be consigned to oblivion. To them we owe our great national game, rugby.

Chapter One

The Mists of Time

I N A SENSE, the beginning of rugby in New Zealand was not an isolated event. Rather, it was part of an amazing sequence of history, in which a game that grew from English village traditions into a unique sports activity then emigrated to New Zealand and other far-flung colonies. It finally established itself as one of the major games on the world sporting scene.

In order to understand the origins of rugby in New Zealand we must first return to England, and journey back through the mists of time, back to the ancient beginnings of football.

Games resembling 'football' were played in several early civilizations, including Egyptian, Greek and Chinese. Most of the indigenous races, including North American Indians, Eskimos, Polynesians, native Filipinos and even the Faroe Islanders, are noted as having their own ethnic games. In New Zealand the Maori enjoyed a game called ki o rahi, played with a woven flax bag that was otherwise used for carrying moa eggs. The Central American Maya Indians played a game that formed part of a religious ritual. After the contest, the captain of the winning team beheaded the captain of the losing side as a sacrifice to the gods.

During the Roman military occupation of Britain, from 43AD to 410AD, the gymnastic game of harpastum, derived from the Greek verb 'to seize', was a popular pastime. It was encouraged by Roman commanders as a means of keeping their men fit and primed for battle. Games were played between garrison soldiers and the local citizenry. Harpastum was probably the first game of any type to be played between two teams on a measured rectangular area. It was usually played with an inflated pig's bladder, the object being to maul, carry, kick or use any means possible to get the bladder into the opponents' goal. It was extremely violent and often resulted in serious physical injury.

A representation of the Roman game of harpastum.
New Zealand Rugby Museum

After the Roman occupation of Britain ended, the written history of Britain virtually ceases for several centuries. It becomes largely an oral history, based on myth and legend. Only the Venerable Bede, in the 8th century, offers any significant written contribution. The first recorded account of football, written in Latin in 1175 by a monk named William Fitzstephen, tells of the youths of London, 'playing with the ball in wide open spaces'.

Football in the 14th century, from the famed misericord at Gloucester Cathedral.

An even earlier traditional account of a contest, played at Chester in pre-Norman times, relates how the game was played with the head of a captured Dane; he was referred to as 'Olaf the Unfortunate'.

The tradition of harpastum had seemingly established itself with the townsfolk in the form of village mauls — games normally played between neighbouring villages. According to folklore, they were usually referred to as 'games of ball' or 'playing at ball'. Unlike harpastum,

An artist's impression of 14th-century 'futeballe'.
Museum of Rugby, Twickenham, England

which had a set number of players, there was no limit on the number of players per side and no defined playing area. Rather, the game was played from one end of the village to the other. There were no obvious rules. The object remained the same: to get the bladder into the opponents' goal by whatever means possible.

Because of their brutality — at least two deaths were recorded after tempers got out of control — the village mauls incurred the ire of various kings and local authorities. They were also seen as a distraction from good bowmanship.

In 1314 King Edward II issued an edict forbidding football: 'Forasmuch as there is a great noise in the city, caused by hustling over large balls from which many evils might arise which God forbid, we commend and forbid, on behalf of the King, on pain of imprisonment, such game to be used in the city in future.'

An edict by Henry VIII in 1531 stated: 'Footeballe, is nothing but beastlie furie and extreme violence, whereof proceedeth hurte . . . wherefore it is to be put in perpetuall silence.' Under Henry VIII and Elizabeth I, a land owner could be fined for allowing football to be played on his land.

The Highways Act of 1835 banned the playing of football on public highways, imposing a maximum penalty of forty shillings.

In 1845 a working man in Derby commented on attempts to ban the annual game: 'It is all disappointment, no sports and no football. This is the way they always treat poor folks.' The following year the authorities in Derby actually called out the troops to prevent the playing of the game.

Despite the attempts at prohibition, the bans were largely ignored. The village mauls continued, and Shrove Tuesday (or Pancake Tuesday), preceding Lent, was established as a popular anniversary for such encounters, particularly around Derbyshire and neighbouring counties. By then, the game was typically referred to as mob football or village football.

The entire town was the playing field, with goals at each end, sometimes as far as 3 miles apart. Damage was frequently inflicted on property as well as on the participants. The ball was usually an inflated pig's bladder or a bundle of rags tied together with twine. The number of players could exceed a thousand and the game might last all day. Men and women, peasants and noblemen, would battle through the streets and fields. Prudent shopkeepers closed their shops, and some even boarded up their windows while the mayhem was afoot.

In most respects, apart from the number of players and the size of the playing area, the village mauls were largely unchanged from Roman harpastum. By 1580, 'football' was tolerated within the colleges at Cambridge University. Later, Oliver Cromwell played 'football' and King Charles II watched his household servants playing the game. The Shrove Tuesday games became increasingly popular and gradually spread to villages all over England.

In 1634, leading dramatist Sir William Davenport holed himself up in a local inn, apprehensive that if he ventured out, he might cop one in the pantaloons. He quilled a message to the local squire: 'I would now make a safe retreat, but methinks I am topped by one of your

Village football in the 18th century, from the painting 'Foot-ball' by noted artist Thomas Webster. The game has not changed over the centuries, although the attire has.

heroic games called footballe which I perceive . . . not very conveniently civil in the streets beneath me. It argues your courage, since you allow such valued exercise in the streets.'

By the 19th century, football was popular everywhere. Although still strongly discouraged, it no longer incurred the wrath of officialdom and some semblance of order was beginning to appear. English novelist Joseph Strutt, in his *Pastimes of the People of England,* published in 1801, described football:

> When match at football is made an equal number of competitors take the field and stand between the goals placed at a distance of eighty or an hundred yards one from the other. The goal is usually made of two sticks driven into the ground about two or three feet apart . . . When the exercise becomes exceedingly violent the players kick each other's shins without the least ceremony, and some of them are overthrown at the hazard of their limbs.

At the beginning of the 19th century most of the public schools of England (there were seven original schools — Winchester, Eton, Harrow, Rugby, Charterhouse, Westminster and Shrewsbury) were beginning to adapt their own versions of village football into their respective institutions. These games were generally organised by the pupils themselves as part of their leisure time activity. Games were often spread over two or three days, with unrestricted numbers of players involved. They were still generally mauling, shoving and kicking encounters, but were largely adapted to suit the location and environment of the particular school.

Rural schools like Shrewsbury and Rugby, with adjoining paddocks and farmland, tended to develop games based around mauling and kicking of the ball. Rugby School was unique in that it had more open space and fields available than any other public school of the time. On the other hand, town schools like Charterhouse, Westminster and Harrow, with only cobblestone courtyards and no soft surfaces, tended to favour a more open kicking type of game. This was to be the basis of things to come. It was the public schools of England that gave the world the early games that ultimately evolved into the modern games of football we have today.

At Rugby School events were to happen that would shape the future.

Summing up in *The Centenary History of the Rugby Football Union,* Ross McWhirter and Uel Titley wrote: 'It can be concluded that some game of ball has existed in Britain at least since Roman times, and although such games have differed somewhat from each other, the common thread has been that they were carrying games.'

Far from the madding crowd's ignoble strife
Their sober wishes never learn'd to stray
Along the cool sequester'd vale of life
They kept the noiseless tenor of their way.

Gray's *Elegy*

Chapter Two

Rugby School

RUGBY FOOTBALL derives its name from Rugby School, the famous English public school. Set in magnificent rural surroundings in Warwickshire, Rugby School was founded and endowed under the will of Lawrence Sherriff, a local grocer and wealthy landowner, in 1567. It is the fourth-oldest public school in England.

In 1823 at Rugby School, a seemingly insignificant event occurred which many regard as the birth of the game of rugby. It is recorded on the famous plaque on Doctor's Wall at Rugby School.

THIS STONE
COMMEMORATES THE EXPLOIT OF
WILLIAM WEBB ELLIS
WHO WITH A FINE DISREGARD FOR THE RULES OF FOOTBALL
AS PLAYED IN HIS TIME
FIRST TOOK THE BALL IN HIS ARMS AND RAN WITH IT
THUS ORIGINATING THE DISTINCTIVE FEATURE OF
THE RUGBY GAME
AD 1823.

The missing word in the eulogy to Ellis is 'forward'. He ran forward with the ball from the mark. Under the unwritten rules of the time, after taking the mark, he should have retired from the mark with the ball, i.e., moved backwards, at which point he could have kicked it wherever he wished or attempted a drop-kick at goal. While it was a definite breach of the rules, it seems that apart from incurring the ire of his schoolmates at the time, the incident was largely forgotten, only to be resurrected some years later.

The main feature of the game at Rugby School around 1823 was the maul, which was not much more than a stacks-on-the-mill mêlée of an indeterminate number of players. The practice of 'hacking', the intentional kicking of opponents' shins in an effort to drive them out of the maul, was common, and the popular cry of the period was: 'Hack him over.' Old Rugbeians were as proud of the scars on their shins, resulting from hacking, as Prussian students were of their duelling scars. They were badges of honour.

The game was called 'football', but when played on the large area of ground on The Close behind the headmaster's garden wall known as Bigside, it was more specifically referred to as 'Bigside' or 'Bigside football'. All major games were played on Bigside. Football was organised and controlled by the pupils. The two captains were the sole arbiters during the game and after each game a levee, or meeting, was held to discuss the game and rule on disputed goals and any other contentious matters.

The game was largely a kicking game — kicking the ball and the opposition in an effort to drive the ball towards the opponents' goal line. There were usually fifty or sixty a side, but it was not uncommon for more than three hundred adversaries to be involved in a game on Bigside, with spectators joining in the legalised mayhem. Numerical equality of the teams was not critical: for example, when School House (seventy-five) played Rest of School (two hundred and fifty) once a year.

When a normal match was to be played, the whole school would assemble and two of the senior players would choose twenty or so colleagues to 'follow up'. The remainder, usually the younger students, referred to as 'fags', were roughly divided into two sides. They were sent to guard the goal and prevent the opposition from crossing the line. Jackets, hats and braces were dumped behind the goalposts, where they remained until play ended. Games often continued, with frequent breaks, for anything up to five days, no side being called at the end of each day. It was not uncommon for players to take time out and sit down for a rest while the game carried on around them.

The object was to drop-kick a field goal or to drive the ball over the opposing team's goal line for a touchdown. Teams strove for a touchdown, which then gave them the right to 'try' to kick a goal by drop-kicking the ball over the goal bar. Games were won by scoring goals, either from the field of play or after a touchdown. After a touchdown the players and spectators would shout, 'A Try, a Try', indicating that an attempt at goal could be made. The word eventually became a key word in rugby parlance.

The plaque on Doctor's Wall, erected 1900.
Rugby School, England

The earliest drawing of a game of Rugby Football depicts Dowager Queen Adelaide and Dr. Thomas Arnold watching, from a distance, a game on the Close in 1839. Between them stands Matthew Arnold, son of Thomas and well-known Victorian poet and educationalist. The match was between School House (75 players) and the Rest (225 players) and Thomas Hughes, later author of "Tom Brown's Schooldays", kicked a goal.

Rugby School, England

Rugby School

A picturecade of Rugby School rugby history

Although published in early 1870 this artist's impression 'Football at Rugby' dates from around 1851. Spectators on the pitch appear to be nothing new!

Rugby School, England

The oldest oil painting of rugby football, depicting a game on The Close in 1859. The view is looking northwest from 'The Island' towards the old chapel and main school building.

Rugby School, England

Contemporary picture of Rugby School.

Rugby School, England

There were no eyewitness accounts of William Webb Ellis's famous exploit, nor is the incident recorded in any contemporary Rugby School chronicle. Even Thomas Hughes, author of the celebrated schoolboy story *Tom Brown's Schooldays*, and Captain of Bigside in 1841–42, makes no mention of the incident, either in his book or in letters he later wrote to the school detailing the history of the game at Rugby during his time.

Was it myth or was it factual? We are reliant on the testimony of Matthew Bloxam, a contemporary of Webb Ellis. Bloxam did not actually see the incident, because he had left Rugby three years earlier, but was apprised of it by an eyewitness. Writing for the school magazine *The Meteor* in 1880, he stated: 'Ellis rushed forward with the ball in his hands towards the opposite goal, with what result to the game, I know not. Neither do I know how this infringement of a well known rule was followed up, or when it became, as it is now, the standing rule.'

After Webb Ellis, the game continued largely unchanged at Rugby for some years, until the rules were eventually changed to permit running forward with the ball, possibly as the

Win or lose, the annual School House versus Rest of School match was celebrated with great gusto in School House.
New Zealand Rugby Museum

result of a Bigside levee decision. The practice became very popular in 1838–39 because of the prowess of the formidable Jem Mackie, the great 'runner-in'. Running in touchdowns was by then an accepted part of the game, but passing the ball was not permitted.

The following extracts from a chapter of *Tom Brown's Schooldays* entitled 'A Bigside at Rugby' illustrate the atmosphere of an annual Bigside match and the colourful language evoked by the occasion:

> . . . the schoolhouse cheers and rush on . . . Then the two sides close, and you can see nothing for minutes but a swaying crowd of boys, at one point violently agitated. That is where the ball is, and there are the keen players to be met, and the glory and the hard knocks to be got. You hear the dull thud of the ball, and the shouts of, 'off your side', 'down with him', 'put him over' and 'bravo'.

Further on Thomas Hughes writes:

> The ball is placed again midway, and the School are going to kick off. Their leaders have sent their lumber into goal, and rated the rest soundly, and one hundred and twenty picked players-up are there, bent on retrieving the game. They are to keep the ball in front of the school-house goal, and then to drive it in by sheer strength

Tom Brown's initiation to football.
New Zealand Rugby Museum

and weight. They mean heavy play, and no mistake, and so old Brooke sees; and places Crab Jones in quarters just before the goal, with four or five picked players, who are to keep the ball away to the sides, where a try at goal, if obtained, will be less dangerous than in front. He himself, and Warner and Hedge, who have saved themselves till now, will lead the charges. 'Are you ready?' 'Yes.' And away comes the ball, kicked high in the air, to give the School time to rush on and catch it as it falls. And here they are amongst us. Meet them like Englishmen, you School-house boys, and charge them home. Now is the time to show what mettle is in you — and there shall be a warm seat by the hall fire, and honour, and lots of bottled beer to-night, for him who does his duty in the next half-hour.

To the Rugby schoolboy of the time, a Bigside football match was an enactment of the English upper-class creed. It embraced a disregard for personal safety and epitomised the doggedness and the pluck that were elemental facets of the English public school spirit and character. It gave physical expression to collective endeavour, and to Christian manliness. Although very combative, there was no malice or aggression. It was a chivalrous contest; but most importantly, it was fun.

In 1845, the first formal written set of rugby rules, thirty-seven in all, entitled 'The Laws of Football', were drawn up for Rugby School by a levee of the sixth, comprising three fifteen-year-old students, William Arnold, Walter Shirley and Frederick Hutchins, and printed in booklet form. The following is a selection from the 1845 rules.

> ## RULE IX
> Charging is fair, in case of a place-kick, as soon as a ball has touched the ground; in case of a kick from a catch, as soon as the player's foot has left the ground and not before.

RULE XVI

A player standing up to another may hold one arm only, but may hack him or knock the ball out of his hand if he attempts to kick it, or go beyond the line of touch.

RULE XX

All matches are drawn after five days, but after three if no goal has been kicked.

RULE XXVI

No hacking with the heel, or above the knee, is fair.

RULE XXX

No player may stop the ball with anything but his own person.

At the same time, in an effort to facilitate player recognition, it was determined for all matches that players on one side should wear white shirts and trousers, while players on the other side should wear striped shirts with white trousers. This is the first recorded use of coloured playing tops. Prior to this, players had to rely on personal recognition.

The game and the rules continued to evolve and change internally at Rugby School, but it wasn't until 1867 that the school played its first 'foreign match', when the School Twenty played A.C. Harrison Esq's Twenty. The Headmaster, Dr Temple, insisted that opposition should be either old Rugbeians or resident, in or near Rugby town. These games became annual fixtures and for the most part were played with twenty players a side.

Arthur Budd, who during the late 1860s was a schoolboy at Clifton College, where the Rugby School game was played, gives the following description of the game as played at that time:

> The arrangement of the field was two full-backs, one three-quarter, two halves and fifteen forwards. It was an act of high treason to put down one's head in the scrummage, and if anybody did so, an opponent would promptly remind him of this breach of etiquette by raising his knee sharply against it. Hacking was permissible, and, as there were no umpires to appeal to in the case of a breach of rules, for example off-side play, the innocent party used to take the law into his own hands, and with a shout of 'off-side sir,' administer the orthodox punishment for the infringement by violently kicking the shin bone of the offender . . . The art of scrummaging consisted of straightforward propulsion. One of those in the front rank was expected to get the ball between his legs, and hold it there tight, while his forwards pushed on him with might and main. The packs frequently lasted two or three minutes, with forwards equipoised; and, to show how times have altered, I have only to mention that in those days the longest scrummage was considered the best.

Rugby School continued to play and modify its own rules until 1881, when it adopted the (English) Rugby Football Union laws. It finally adopted the fifteen-a-side game for Bigside matches in 1883 and affiliated with the Rugby Football Union in 1892. Throughout the period, rugby football remained very much an internal game at Rugby, with the continuing focus on 'foreign' matches, Bigside matches and house matches.

It wasn't until 1896 that Rugby School played its first inter-school match, against Cheltenham College. At the turn of the century, Uppingham School became the other regular opposition.

Perhaps the final act in the great Rugby School saga of the 19th century was the establishment in 1895 of the Sub-Committee to Enquire into the Origin of Rugby Football. The committee, comprising four old Rugbeians, sat intermittently for almost two years. It reviewed the written material submitted by Matthew Bloxam to *The Meteor* in 1880, along with information from other old Rugbeians, including two lengthy submissions from Thomas Hughes, written two years before he died.

Apart from piecing together the largely hitherto unwritten history of rugby at Rugby School and reaching other conclusions, the committee ratified the evidence of Matthew Bloxam concerning William Webb Ellis running forward with the ball. And so, more than seventy years after the event, the second-hand account was accepted and the episode became part of rugby lore. The greatest sporting legend since Phidippides the Greek heroically ran from Marathon to Sparta was born.

During this period, other events occurred outside Rugby School that led to the development and establishment of the Rugby School game throughout England.

Rupert Brooke, the brilliant young poet and patriot who became a national hero when he died at the age of twenty-eight in 1915, attended Rugby School at the beginning of the 20th century. He wrote the following light-hearted poem about his initial experience of playing rugby:

When first I played I nearly died
The bitter memory still rankles —
They formed a scrum with me inside!
Some kicked the ball and some my ankles.
I did not like the game at all
Yet, after all the harm they'd done me,
Whenever I came near the ball,
They knocked me down and stood on me.

Rupert Brooke

William Webb Ellis

WILLIAM WEBB ELLIS was born at Salford, Manchester, on 24 November 1806. After the death of his father at the battle of Albuera in 1812, his widowed mother moved with her two sons to Rugby town, to a location within 10 miles of the Rugby clock tower so she would not have to pay tuition fees. Webb Ellis entered Rugby School in 1816 at the age of nine, as a town boy. He was only sixteen when he incurred the displeasure of his team-mates by running forward with the ball from the mark. He made no other significant contribution to life at Rugby School or to the game of rugby, and quite possibly never even handled a rugby ball again.

A contemporary of Webb Ellis, at Rugby School, a Mr T. Harris, related: 'I remember William Webb Ellis perfectly. He was an admirable cricketer but was generally inclined to take unfair advantages at football.'

Webb Ellis went on to Oxford University, where he took Holy Orders in preparation for entering the church. In 1827 he won a cricket blue playing against Cambridge University in the world's first inter-university sports fixture of any kind. He lived out an upright life as rector at St Clement Danes in London (now the chapel of the Royal Air Force), and spent his last seventeen years at Magdalene Laver parish in Essex, where there is a Webb Ellis stained-glass window.

The only known portrait of William Webb Ellis. Published by the *Illustrated London News* on the occasion of a sermon he delivered during the Crimean War.
New Zealand Rugby Museum

He died in 1872, probably of tuberculosis, a year after the founding of the Rugby Football Union. His death remained a mystery until 1959, when his grave was discovered by Ross McWhirter in the Vieux Château cemetery at Menton, on the French Riviera. McWhirter had been commissioned by the Rugby Football Union to find Webb Ellis's grave. The grave has since become a shrine, a Mecca for rugby devotees the world over.

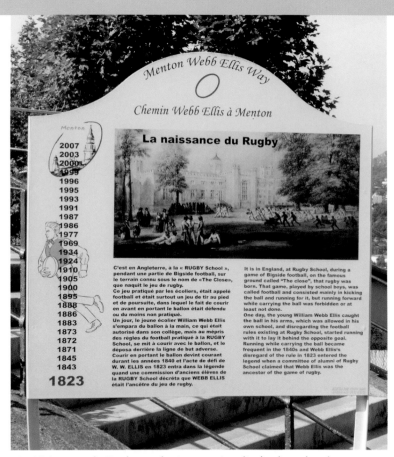

La Naissance du Rugby — the interpretive display board at the entrance to the cemetery at Vieux Château, Menton, France.
Mark Holmes

A place of pilgrimage. The grave of William Webb Ellis at the cemetery of Vieux Châteaux, Menton, France.

Keith Quinn

Webb Ellis never knew that he was to become a sporting legend. As best we know, he never personally received any accolades or recognition. All his tributes have been posthumous — even the famous plaque on Doctor's Wall at Rugby School was not put in place until 1900, twenty-eight years after his death. He remained largely forgotten until the old Rugbeians committee, sitting in 1895–96, bestowed on him a place in history. There is still considerable debate as to whether Webb Ellis even made such a vaunted dash with the ball. Was it just an old school yarn, a piece of rugby folklore, or did it really happen?

Still, whether deserved or not, Webb Ellis has been given an exalted place in rugby tradition. No other sports code today can boast such an iconic figure. Rugby has a unique heritage. The rugby World Cup is named after William Webb Ellis, an indication of his conferred status and of his place in the history of the game.

Chapter Three

The Oval Ball

The development of the oval rugby ball parallels the development of the game of rugby. The commemorative plaque on Doctor's Wall at Rugby School fails to mention that the ball carried forward by William Webb Ellis was probably a Gilbert ball. About the time that Webb Ellis was at Rugby School, William Gilbert (1799–1877) opened a boot and shoemaker's shop in the High Street, Rugby, next to the school, and started making balls for the school. The balls were hand-stitched, four-panel leather casings supported by an inflated pig's bladder. The Gilbert ball was to become synonymous with rugby and evolved with the game, in response to the changing needs of the game it served.

The ball commonly used in England in the early 19th century was round. Early leather-cased balls were probably part of the local village cobbler's trade in England even before William Gilbert's time. The Gilbert ball was not the first leather-cased ball and there are suggestions that such balls might have been made by village cobblers as far back as the Elizabethan period. However, it is apparent that by the time Gilbert set up business it was the practice to place the traditional inflated pig's bladder inside a leather casing — perhaps to afford it some protection, perhaps to mitigate the smell!

At Rugby School the ball was always fairly oval-shaped. Thomas Hughes, in *Tom Brown's Schooldays*, discusses a game on Bigside in 1835 and refers to the ball being less rounded at the ends and pointing towards the school goal. Early drawings also support this. The balls varied in size and shape, depending on the size and shape of the pig's bladder; the leather casings were made to fit individual bladders.

Gilbert used to journey far afield from Rugby in search of the none-too-savoury pigs' bladders. The bladder, still in its smelly raw state, would be placed inside the specially crafted leather casing or outer. It was then inflated by lung power down the stem of a clay pipe inserted in the neck of the bladder. The balls were then laced and hung up to cure until ready for use.

James Gilbert, 'a wonder of lung strength'.
Museum of Rugby, Twickenham, England

William Gilbert was joined in the business by his nephew James Gilbert (1831–1906), who was reputed to be a wonder of lung strength who blew even the big match balls up tight. He was also noted for his trade in 'tweakers' (catapults) of rare power and precision. He supplied these to the Rugby School boys until banned by the school authorities. James Gilbert produced an oval-shaped ball that was exhibited in the 1851 Great London Exhibition, where it was awarded a prize medal. This was the first popular rugby ball and was generally used by rugby-playing football clubs from this point on. There was still no standardisation of the size, shape or weight of the ball.

Old Rugbeian E.T. Bennett wrote about the ball as played with during the 1860s. 'The shape of our ball came from the bladder and was a perfect ball for long drop-kicking or placing and for dribbling too. The modern plumstone is good for none of these.'

Around 1862, a major development occurred when another ball maker from Rugby town, Richard Lyndon, developed the idea of making bladders out of rubber. In 1875 he invented a brass hand pump for inflating the balls and went on to develop a somewhat over-large foot pump. Lyndon later claimed to have invented the oval-shaped rugby ball but, sadly for him, he failed to patent neither the ball, the bladder, nor his pumps. By the 1880s there were several manufacturers of 'footballs' in England, all using the same process. Whether Gilbert and Lyndon were friends and co-operated together is not known.

Although a vast improvement over the old pig's bladder, the rubber bladders were individually made and difficulties remained in achieving consistency of quality and shape. However, it was an important breakthrough, and *The Rugby Advertiser* of 28 January 1871 recorded: 'Our townsman Mr Gilbert has sent to Australia this week twenty dozen [240] of his celebrated footballs as used at Rugby School.' Very soon the Gilbert ball was being sent to all the world's rugby-playing countries, albeit with different panel designs and configurations. It quickly became the internationally accepted rugby ball.

The name Gilbert will always be associated with the rugby ball and rugby football. William Gilbert, a bachelor, died at the age of seventy-seven and was succeeded in the business by James Gilbert. He in turn was succeeded by his son, James John, who was succeeded by his son James, the fourth generation Gilbert, and the last family member to be involved in the company. Since then the company has passed through different hands, but has continued to proudly uphold the Gilbert name and tradition and the incomparable standard of the Gilbert rugby ball.

The rugby ball went through a continuing process of shape evolution and it wasn't until 1892 that the Rugby Football Union fixed the first standard dimensions for the ball. Charles MacIntosh and Company was the first firm to supply rubber

Richard Lyndon's 1875 brass hand pump for inflation of rugby footballs. The foot pump was a later invention and used until 1930.
Rugby School, England

bladders in sufficient numbers to make standardisation possible. The following year, four-panel balls were determined as a universal standard. The shape of the ball continued to become more oval as the game changed from a predominantly kicking game to a handling one, until the modern synthetic ball finally emerged. Today, the Gilbert ball is the most universally used rugby ball in the world, and continues to be subjected to technical improvements.

On the ball, on the ball
Through scrimmage, three quarters and all
Sticking together, we keep on the leather
And shout as we go, 'on the ball'.

E.W. Secker

The oldest known rugby ball.
Rugby School, England

William Gilbert's shop in St Matthews Street, now the Gilbert Museum.
Rugby School, England

Football in England — Timeline

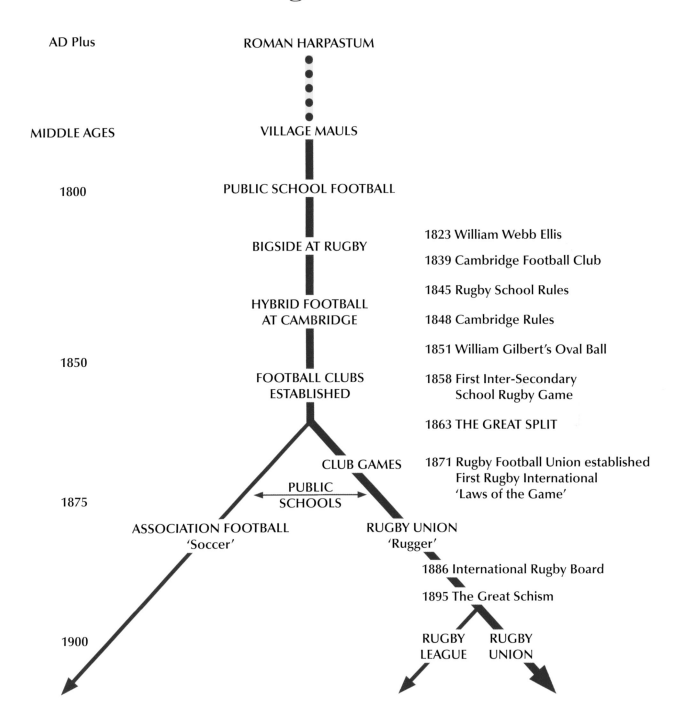

AD Plus — ROMAN HARPASTUM

MIDDLE AGES — VILLAGE MAULS

1800 — PUBLIC SCHOOL FOOTBALL

BIGSIDE AT RUGBY — 1823 William Webb Ellis

1839 Cambridge Football Club

1845 Rugby School Rules

HYBRID FOOTBALL AT CAMBRIDGE — 1848 Cambridge Rules

1851 William Gilbert's Oval Ball

1850 — FOOTBALL CLUBS ESTABLISHED — 1858 First Inter-Secondary School Rugby Game

1863 THE GREAT SPLIT

CLUB GAMES — 1871 Rugby Football Union established First Rugby International 'Laws of the Game'

PUBLIC SCHOOLS

1875 — ASSOCIATION FOOTBALL 'Soccer' — RUGBY UNION 'Rugger'

1886 International Rugby Board

1895 The Great Schism

1900 — RUGBY LEAGUE — RUGBY UNION

Chapter Four

England's Green and Pleasant Land

INHERENT IN the nature of man is the need for physical exertion. This often finds expression in the form of competition or sports contests with people of like mind. The young men emerging from the public schools of England in the early part of the 18th century were no different in this respect. Many had a common interest in football, but they were faced with a problem; they were products of schools that played completely different versions of football.

There were early efforts at games of football between former students of the public schools, particularly at Cambridge University. These could best be described as hybrid versions of football, incorporating elements of different public school games. There was little standardisation and rules varied markedly. Normally the rules would be decided by the team captains after a wrangle before the game started. In one game at Cambridge during this period, between old Etonians and old Rugbeians, the Etonians were dumbfounded and irate when the Rugbeians took every opportunity to handle and run with the ball.

There were no referees and the games were under the control of the two captains. All too often their communications were indecisive, leading to misunderstandings and bad feelings on the pitch. Fundamental differences were always apparent, particularly over issues like dribbling, handling and hacking.

In 1839, former Rugbeian Arthur Pell attempted to establish the Rugby School game at Cambridge University. Unfortunately, football generally was not recognised by the university authorities, although it continued to be played and proved popular with the undergraduates. As a result, the distinction of being the world's first rugby football club was claimed by the Guy's Hospital club, which was reputedly established in 1843. However, doubts have arisen over whether Guy's Hospital was actually playing the Rugby School game at this time. Present-day rugby historians now generally accept that Liverpool, established in 1857, was the first club to play the Rugby School game.

The idea that the form of football introduced by Arthur Pell was to be rugby football became clouded by the involvement of old Salopians (Shrewsbury School) and old Etonians (Eton College), who completely disparaged handling and running with the ball, but were a major part of the football scene at Cambridge. This led to games continuing to be played under different rules, often depending on the composition of the teams for the particular game. An early attempt was made to draw up a set of common rules to be fair to all schools, without any apparent general acceptance.

However, Cambridge University was to become the focal point of football in 1848 when the first serious attempt to establish a uniform set of rules met with success. A fourteen-man committee of public school and non-public school men, including old Rugbeians, endured prolonged debate to draw up the 'Cambridge rules', an 'amalgamation of all forms of football'. There was considerable disagreement over many issues, and the divisions remained.

The original Cambridge rules, long since lost, were incorporated in a further set of rules in the late 1850s. By this time, football clubs like Guy's Hospital, Liverpool, Manchester, Blackheath, Richmond and Sale were being established by former public school men. Some clubs played the Cambridge rules, some Rugby School rules (or variations of the same); some, such as London Rovers, sponsored both sets of rules, and some used other public school rules.

As a result of this continuing division, different factions emerged. On one hand there were the so-called 'dribbling men', and on the other there were the 'handling men'. The situation was further complicated by the issue of whether to allow hacking and 'running in' touchdowns.

The disunity came to a head in 1863. A series of meetings was held between representatives of the football clubs, in order to form a football association and to reach agreement on the rules. Until this time, despite the considerable differences, all parties had genuinely been seeking compromise and agreement. At the sixth meeting, held on 1 December 1863, the Football Association was formed. Then, as a result of last-minute manoeuvres, the clubs supporting dribbling reached a consensus and opted for the Cambridge rules. Clubs supporting the Cambridge rules and those supporting the Rugby School game met head on — the Cambridge faction won the critical decision, by a vote of 13–4.

There had been heated debate during the meetings over the dribbling versus handling issue, but more particularly over the practice of hacking. Twenty-year-old Francis Campbell, representing the recently formed Blackheath Club, argued that hacking was an essential element of football and that to eliminate it would 'do away with all the courage and pluck from the game, and I will be bound over to bring over a lot of Frenchmen who would beat you with a week's practice'. Personal insults were traded and at the final meeting held on 8 December Campbell stormed out and took the handling men with him. The final split between the dribbling men and the handling men had occurred. Ironically, Blackheath outlawed hacking two years later.

Francis Campbell of Blackheath — the man whose obstinacy led to rugby being established as a separate game.
Museum of Rugby, Twickenham, England

We can only wonder what sort of game might have evolved if Francis Campbell had not walked out of that 1863 meeting. But for his conviction and obstinacy, we could have all been playing entirely different versions of football today.

Some efforts were made to retrieve the situation,

but English football had split irretrievably. From this point, the two factions became separate games and began to move in different directions. Called rugby football and association football, in short time a new vernacular emerged, 'rugger' and 'soccer'. (The word 'soccer' is derived from the word 'association'.)

There were still huge changes in store. Neither game was recognisable with its modern counterpart. Soccer, with its own set of rules and an administrative organisation in place, began to establish a pathway to the future. Rugby, on the other hand, was going nowhere, with different versions of the rules being played, no governing or co-ordinating body and little or no cohesion between the rugby-playing clubs.

After the 1863 split, clubs playing the Rugby School rules, or versions of the same, continued to play internal games between different combinations of their club members. In 1865 the two great clubs, Blackheath and Richmond, played the first recorded interclub rugby match.

Other rugby clubs gradually followed suit and began to play games against each other, usually on a challenge basis. True, rugby was now a distinct game in its own right, but it functioned only on an ad hoc basis. Interclub matches were at best irregular, and playing opportunity was limited, with most clubs having restricted membership. The control of games remained in the hands of the captains, a practice which led to a lot of jawing and arguments. Sometimes a captain would give in just to get some more play, while in other situations, extra time would be added to make up for the lost play.

It was also during this period that interest in village mauls or mob football began to wane, although a few fixtures, local traditions, still continue to be played today. England was going through the industrial revolution and was changing from an agrarian village society to an industrial urban society. One of the results was a dramatic increase in the demand for education. To the traditional core of public schools existing in the middle of the 19th century, a number of new schools were added. In due course, masters from Rugby School found themselves appointed to these schools and the Rugby ethos became implanted in them, not only scholastically, but also in the area of sport.

New public schools like Marlborough, Cheltenham, Uppingham, Clifton, Haileybury, Sherborne and Wellington, along with Rugby, were to be the nursery for the growth of rugby. It was these schools that were to blaze the rugby trail. At the same time, after the 1863 split, the old public schools like Harrow, Eton and Winchester were beginning to abandon their own in-school games, most of them aligning themselves with association football.

The first inter-secondary school rugby match was played between Edinburgh Academy and Merchiston Castle School in Scotland in 1858 and the first inter-secondary school match in England was played between Clifton College and Marlborough College in 1864. This was eventually followed by other inter-school matches in England and Wales. Secondary school rugby was slowly beginning to establish itself and in so doing, provided the platform upon which the game would be built.

The formation of the Rugby Football Union in 1871 was triggered by a letter from Edwin Ash, secretary of the Richmond club, and B.H. Burns, secretary of Blackheath, to the London press. The letter stated:

> An opinion has for sometime prevailed among the supporters of Rugby football, that some code should be adopted by all clubs who profess to play the rugby game, as at present the majority have altered in some slight manner the game as played at Rugby School by introducing new rules of their own . . . We therefore propose that all clubs playing the rugby game will join us in forming a code to be generally adopted. Secretaries of clubs approving of this will greatly oblige by forwarding their names to us.

At the time there were seventy-five clubs playing the Rugby School game in England.

A meeting was called as a result of this letter. It was held on 26 January 1871 in the Pall Mall restaurant at 1 Cockspur Street, near Trafalgar Square, London, and was chaired by E.C. Holmes of the Richmond club. Twenty-one clubs sent a total of thirty-two delegates. Most of them were young men in their twenties. One delegate, from the Wasps club, did not make the meeting. Story has it that he mistakenly entered a nearby hostelry from which, owing to some steady imbibing, he failed to emerge!

The decision to form the Rugby Football Union was passed unanimously and a committee was formed — the word 'English' was not and never has been part of the formal title. The whole meeting took only two hours. Old Rugbeians, Algernon Rutter and Edwin Ash, both of Richmond, were appointed president and

The old Pall Mall Restaurant in Cockspur Street where the Rugby Football Union was born in 1871.
Museum of Rugby, Twickenham, England

honorary secretary, respectively. At the same time, a committee of three old Rugbeians — Rutter, Holmes and Leonard Maton — was appointed to draft a standard set of rules for use by all clubs. The new rules, fifty-nine in all, were entitled 'Laws of the Game'. All three being lawyers, they used the term 'Laws' in preference to 'Rules'. The laws were based on the Rugby School rules, apart from six variations, one of which was the abolition of hacking.

In a letter to the *Morning Post*, published just before he died in 1933, Maton confessed that the laws were entirely of his composition. Having being laid up with a broken leg, caused by playing rugby, Maton was delegated the laborious task of completing the draft. His two colleagues supplied him with free

Algernon Rutter, first president of the Rugby Football Union.
Museum of Rugby, Twickenham, England

Leonard Maton, who drafted the 'Laws of the Game'.
Museum of Rugby, Twickenham, England

tobacco in return for his efforts. When he finished, they approved his work and the laws were subsequently adopted in their entirety at a special meeting of the Rugby Football Union, held on 24 June 1871. The fact that Maton alone had drafted the laws remained a secret for more than sixty years.

On 27 March 1871, the first international football match in the world of any type was played. It was a twenty-a-side rugby match between England and Scotland. The game was organised by the English rugby clubs, in response to a challenge issued in two London newspapers by the leading Scottish clubs. It was played on The Edinburgh Academy cricket field at Raeburn Place, Edinburgh, before 4000 spectators. The Scots won by a goal and a try to a solitary try scored by England. Referees were not introduced to rugby until 1875, but this game was 'umpired' by Hely Almond, later headmaster of the famous Loretto School.

The 1871 England side which played the first international versus Scotland. The ball is still spherical.
Museum of Rugby, Twickenham, England

In 1872, in a touch of historical irony, rugby was recognised by the Cambridge University authorities. Thirty-three years after Arthur Pell's attempt to establish rugby football at Cambridge, the Cambridge Rugby Football Club was formally established and became a member of the Rugby Football Union.

Over the next few years rugby grew steadily if not spectacularly. The advent of the Rugby Football Union and the introduction of standard rules helped the game to take root. In 1875, fifteen-a-side was adopted, referees began to appear and new rules were introduced to provide for different ways of scoring. Until this time, teams were generally twenty-a-side and the only way of scoring was by kicking a goal after a try, or directly off the ground during open play — a field goal.

Commercialism had begun to creep into English rugby, probably prior to 1880.

The Rugby School game had been basically an enormous moving scrum with lots of booting the ball forward on the odd occasion it came loose. Handling became a distinctive feature of rugby football during the late 1870s, as back play became more organised and passing the ball was no longer seen as a cowardly way of avoiding being tackled. The modern game was beginning to emerge.

The Club

No RUGBY CLUB has contributed more to the establishment of rugby in England than Blackheath, often referred to as 'The Club'.

Blackheath was purportedly founded in 1858 by old boys of Blackheath Proprietary School. The club originally played Harrow school rules and was the first club in the world without restricted membership. In 1862, Blackheath established its own code or explanation of football rules, which included the famous rule ten: 'Though it is lawful to hold any player in a scrimmage, this does not include attempts to throttle or strangle, which are totally opposed to the spirit of the game.'

In 1863 Blackheath was a founder member of the Football Association, but, under the leadership of Francis Campbell, withdrew from the association over the issue of hacking, and laid the seeds for the establishment of the rugby game.

From this point Blackheath assumed a leadership role among the rugby-playing football clubs. In 1865, it played the first interclub rugby match, against Richmond, and this is now the oldest regular fixture played in rugby football. In December 1870, Blackheath and Richmond were instrumental in calling the meeting of rugby-playing clubs that led to the formation of the Rugby Football Union. A few months later, Blackheath assisted in organising the first rugby international match, England versus Scotland on 27 March 1871.

One of the great clubs of English rugby, Blackheath played a positive role in the development of the game. Before the establishment of Twickenham in 1907, a number of internationals, as well as the annual Oxford versus Cambridge matches, were played on Rectory Field, the Blackheath ground. It was a Blackheath official, William Carpmael, who founded the Barbarians Club, the world's most celebrated occasional team.

Blackheath is one of eight of the original twenty-one clubs that set up the Rugby Football Union that survives today, and over the years has contributed more than 250 players to international teams, including England captains. The club's emblem is a stylised sprig of gorse or 'whin', a reminder of its origins on the heath. Today, when cheering for their team, Blackheath supporters simply call: 'The Club, The Club.'

Footnote: In 1988 Blackheath made a short tour of New Zealand, courtesy of the Christchurch Football Club, which was celebrating its 125th anniversary.

The oldest picture of a Blackheath team, circa 1860.
Christchurch Football Club

In a sense there had been two separate contributors to the evolution of rugby in England. On one hand, there was the development of the game within Rugby School itself, and on the other, there was the wider community growth of the game, led by the new public schools and emerging rugby football clubs. By 1873, all these English interests were largely united in their approach to the game. In 1873, Charles Alcock's *Football Annual* recorded fifty-three clubs and schools playing association, eighty-one playing rugby union, and sixteen playing the rules in place at Rugby School.

Rugby by this time was also well established in Scotland, Wales and Ireland, and in 1886 these three countries formed the International Rugby Football Board. England initially declined to join.

A drawing of the first international club match between Rosslyn Park and a Paris team, circa 1880.
Museum of Rugby, Twickenham, England

It might have been expected that the Rugby Football Union would have taken a positive lead in helping English rugby to grow. In fact, the opposite happened. Having put the laws in place, they then did very little. There was no attempt to organise any form of club championships or competitions. Only in the north of England, where the Yorkshire Cup was contested by northern clubs, did any meaningful competition occur. This was to lead to the 'great schism' and the formation of the Northern Union (rugby league) in 1895.

Rugby union remained elitist and conservative, very much the property of the largely autonomous clubs, most of which still had restricted or limited membership. Interclub fixtures were arranged by the clubs themselves and consisted of knockout competitions organised on a county basis, or of one-off challenge matches. Rugby was very much the gentlemen's social game, played not too seriously and without any thought of reward or recognition, espousing the doctrine of muscular Christianity.

Soccer, on the other hand, opened its game to the masses, introduced professionalism and instituted club championships that remain the hallmark of the game today. It was a loss of opportunity from which rugby in England never fully recovered. It was to be another hundred years before English rugby began to finally stir itself from its entrenched ideas and practices.

At this point we take leave of England's Green and Pleasant Land to continue the rugby saga elsewhere. The game that England gave birth to, nurtured and shaped, had by this time been introduced to New Zealand. This is where our attention now focuses.

Where shall the watchful sun
England, my England
Match the master work you've done
England my own
When shall he rejoice again
Such a breed of mighty men.

William Henley

The Eton Wall Game

THE ETON WALL GAME has to be one of the oddities of the sports world. It is one of the few original public school games still played as a celebration of school tradition. Eton College has long since abandoned its much acclaimed 'field game' in favour of soccer and rugby, but the Wall Game, described as a ritual for ritual's sake, continues as an anachronistic observance of deep-rooted school tradition. The most important fixture is the annual St Andrew's Day match between 'Collegers' and 'Oppidans'.

The game is played alongside a brick wall built in 1717, on a strip of ground 5 metres wide and 110 metres long. There are eighteen or twenty players per side for normal matches, except for the St Andrew's Day match, when the Collegers, limited to scholarship holders, play the Oppidans, comprising most of the rest of the school.

It takes the form of a prolonged and extremely arduous rugby scrummage, called a 'bully'. Every effort is made to force the ball towards the opponent's goal. Once the ball is driven into the last few metres of the playing strip, an area known as the calx, the attacking side can attempt to gain a shy, worth one point, by lifting the ball against the wall with a player's foot. If successful, a throw at goal (a garden door at one end and a tree trunk at the other), worth nine points if scored, can then be made.

The game lasts up to an hour, thirty minutes per half, with many games ending scoreless. Scoring goals is very rare — the last goal in the St Andrew's Day game was in 1909. The rules are complicated and quirky and the game is a tedious, indecisive parody in which huge amounts of physical energy are expended, usually for little or no gain. One writer described the Wall Game as a game where goals are scored with inspiring regularity once every twenty-five years.

In the 2002 St Andrew's Day match, the Oppidans won by two shies to nil, with Prince Harry, son of the Prince of Wales, scoring one of the shies.

Other surviving public school games still played on special occasions are Harrow Footer and Winchester Football.

The early Eton Wall Game: the two sides involved are distinguished by their jerseys and spectators have made their appearance.

The modern Eton Wall Game — 'a ritual for ritual's sake'.

Chapter Five

Before Rugby in New Zealand

THERE WAS a short time in New Zealand's early colonial history when sport hardly figured in our social pastimes. The early whalers, settlers and military of New Zealand were mostly preoccupied with other things. Maori, on the other hand, enjoyed canoe racing, poi dancing, traditional hand games and ki o rahi. However, soon the sporting instincts of the early settlers began to stir.

Some of the first sports activities centred around anniversary day celebrations, when regattas using ships' boats, fencing and cutlass practice, musket-firing, foot races and dancing 'to the music of the fife, fiddle and drum' were popular fare.

Horse racing and cricket were the first organised sports to appear. The personal horses of gentlemen settlers were used for early horse races. The first recorded horse race took place at the Te Aro Pa, Wellington, in 1841 and later that year the Auckland Town Plate was run at Epsom for a purse of three guineas. The first organised game of cricket took place at Nelson on New Year's Day, 1842, between survey cadets and artisans of the New Zealand Company. They used bats, balls and stumps that they had brought from England. Further games at Nelson and Wellington followed the same year.

It is possible that informal games of football took place at an early stage in our colonial history. The first recorded football match of any type in New Zealand, as reported in the

Lyttelton Times, was played in Christchurch on 16 December 1854, as part of the fourth anniversary celebrations of the Christchurch settlement. No description of the game was given. It was very likely a light-hearted affair played with a round ball, without much attention being given to any rules.

As had happened in England, it was a secondary school that laid the foundation for the establishment of structured football in New Zealand — in this case, Christ's College, Canterbury. Christ's College, New Zealand's oldest secondary school, was established in Lyttelton in 1851 as an Anglican school under the auspices of the Canterbury Association. The following year the college shifted to a site at St Michael's parsonage in Christchurch, and the boys petitioned the Superintendent of Canterbury, John Robert Godley, for 'a portion of land for a playground, where we may be able to play at cricket and football'. Godley replied that he had appropriated an acre of land close to the school for that purpose. In 1857 the college shifted to its present site in Rolleston Avenue.

Christ's College, Rolleston Avenue, Christchurch, circa 1857.
Christ's College Archives

In his reminiscences, Charles Dudley, a pupil at Christ's College from 1853 to 1860, recalled how the boys cleared tussock from a gully at the back of St Michael's Church to fashion a field for cricket and football. When the school moved into the new buildings, they again cleared tussock from a paddock on the east side of Rolleston Avenue, known as Raven's Paddock, for cricket and football. But on great occasions football was played on an area where AMI Stadium (formerly Lancaster Park) is now situated. Dudley further relates: 'For footballs, at first we had bullocks' bladders covered with leather. It was a mixed sort of game brought down by the Wellington boys . . . When Mr Croisdale [sic] Bowen, then a student in the Upper Department and an old Rugby boy, tried to teach us the rugby game, the boys would not have it, and hacked him.' This occurred before 1857.

Another recollection, from Edward Dobson, a pupil at Christ's College from 1861 to 1863, stated that 'football was played at Christ's College a long time before recognised rules were drawn up'. These rules were written in 1862 and, with the additions that were passed by the Games Committee from time to time, formed the basis of Christ's College football for many years to come.

In 1860 an informal game of football was played by Christchurch citizens on Kiver's Paddock and in 1862 a similar type of game was played between citizens of Christchurch and Lyttelton at Charteris Bay. The first organised match was played at Latimer Square in June 1862, when a team of twenty-two Christ's College Fellows and Pupils played the Townspeople of Christchurch. From these games a nucleus of players was established, many of them former Christ's College boys, who became the pioneer members of the Christchurch Football Club.

Meanwhile, an event occurred at Nelson College in 1860, the significance of which has never been fully realised. Nelson College, founded in 1856, was New Zealand's third secondary school, and at the time was still in temporary premises in Manuka Street. Officiating in Nelson at the time were two Anglican clergymen, Robert Codrington and Henry Turton. Both were English public school old boys and the 1909 *Nelson College Old Boys Register* comments that 'they taught the Collegians the game, but it did not become popular until a much later date'.

An old boy writing under the nom de plume 'Scrum' for the September 1910 *Nelsonian* relates the following account of a game of 'football' played in a paddock in Brook Street in 1860 between a School Eighteen and the Rest of the School:

> After being marshalled into sundry positions and instructions given, we started play, and then the fun commenced in real earnest. The Rest of the School just simply swarmed over us like flies over a honey pot. No one was very particular about whether it was the ball or some schoolfellow's head, shins, or any other part of his body, so long as he got a kick in. The whistle shrieked, but our blood was up and we were not going to stop for such a trifle as that. After careering over and around the field, by the aid of the masters and coaches (they were hopelessly mixed up with us) they did manage at last to separate us; but we were panting for the blood of the Rest of the School. Result of first spell: nil.
>
> At the beginning of the second spell the tables were turned. The Rest of the School had extended themselves too much in the first spell, so down they went like nine-pins, but we could not get that ball through or over the bar, and the battle ended (so the referee said) in a draw. Final result: Eighteen men bandaging legs, ankles, and heads, and the masters were so ashamed of our dilapidated appearance that they gave us a holiday the next day to get over the battle.

'Scrum' records that the coaches were Reverends Codrington and Turton.

The fact that the sides were of uneven strength, and references to 'kicks in the shin', 'down like ninepins', and 'over the bar', give a clear indication that this was an attempt to replicate a game of Bigside football, as played at Rugby

The Reverend A.C. Codrington. Did he introduce the game of rugby into New Zealand?
Nelson Diocesan Trust

School at this time. The unavoidable conclusion is that a game akin to rugby was played in Nelson ten years before the first recognised match in 1870. 'Scrum' concludes his article with the comment, 'I have wondered many times of recent years when watching football, what game we really did play.' An early *Nelsonian* described the contest as resembling the famous match, Schoolhouse versus School, of *Tom Brown's Schooldays*.

Soon after the match, Reverends Codrington and Turton were both transferred away from Nelson and no further games of this type were played.

In Christchurch, important developments were taking place. On 26 August 1863, a football match was played at Cranmer Square between Christ's College and Twenty-two Gentlemen of the town. After the match a club of gentlemen was formed; the Christchurch Football Club. The committee comprised young Christchurch notables, and one of the vice-presidents was the ubiquitous Rev. Croasdaile Bowen. The Christchurch Football Club thus became the first football club of any sort to be formed in New Zealand, although at this stage it was not a rugby football club. The club adopted the colours of red and white and established its own set of rules, a mixture of association football and Victorian rules (see Chapter 13). Once again hacking was expressly forbidden.

Although the Christchurch club's game differed slightly from the Christ's College game, particularly as far as the Victorian rules content applied, the two organisations were able to compromise and enjoy regular fixtures against each other until

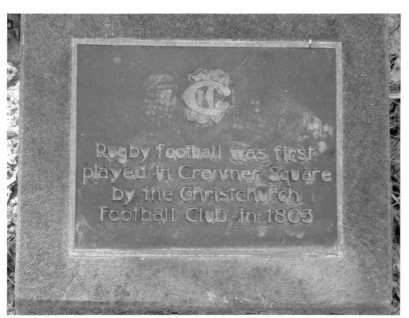

A stone cairn in Cranmer Square, Christchurch, placed by persons unknown, commemorating a supposed game of rugby played in 1863.

1875. Another early opponent of the club was the Lyttelton Football Club (1864–67, 1870–73), until it became defunct in 1873. This left the Christchurch Football Club playing a lot of internal games between different combinations of its own club members.

In 1873 former English public schoolboy Montague Lewin arrived in Christchurch. He later related: 'I found the club playing a regular "all sorts" of rules, bouncing the ball every four yards after the Australian rules. It was quite a common thing to find the game held up for several minutes to allow argument to take place.' However, by the early 1870s an increasing number of men who had played rugby in England began joining the Christchurch club and practices akin to the Rugby School game began to be incorporated into the local game. By August 1871, goals were permitted to be scored by either rugby or soccer methods, and between 1872 and 1874 players began scrimmaging and handling the ball.

After his first game with the club, Lewin, along with old Rugbeian Charles Boulton, moved that the Rugby Football Union rules be adopted by the club. They were beaten decisively on the vote. The following season they got together a team of players who had played rugby in England and challenged the club to a match under rugby rules. On 29 May 1874, the Christchurch Football Club played its first rugby match under Rugby Football Union rules. After playing the touring Auckland Provincial Clubs team at rugby in 1875, the club formally adopted rugby from the beginning of the 1876 season.

A small wall plaque at the Royal Hotel, Nelson commemorating the founding of the Nelson Football Club in 1868.

An important event occurred in Nelson on 30 May 1868. At the initiative of Robert Tennent, a local bank clerk, the Nelson Football Club was formed. The club's football was also of a hybrid type — a mixture of soccer and Victorian rules. The *Nelson Examiner* commented: 'A football club has been formed in Nelson which we hope to see prosper as we do all sports which promote healthful exercise.' The club was destined in 1870 to become the Nelson Rugby Football Club, the first rugby club in New Zealand.

The association between the Nelson Football Club and Nelson College had an early beginning. The *Nelson Examiner* of 23 June 1869 commented on a 'football' match played the previous Saturday, between 'sixteen of the College and sixteen of the Nelson Club . . . From the first it was seen that the Collegians had more wind than their opponents and were in better practice. After a long struggle of nearly two hours a goal was kicked for College by F.B. Wither . . . thus ended the first football match played in the Nelson Province.' The *Examiner* subsequently reported on three further matches played between the two teams during the same season, with the townsmen defeating their youthful opponents in the final game.

In other centres, other 'football' events were taking place. W.W. Robinson, a footballer of the period, recalled seeing a crowd of all sorts punting a small black football around in the Auckland Domain as early as 1868. The first recorded match in Auckland was between a party of Jack Tars (sailors) from HMS *Rosario* and local citizens at the Albert Barracks in June 1870. It rained 'pitchforks and rivulets', the rules were of a nondescript sort and even the players were not sure who won. Later that year an Auckland team visited Thames aboard the steamer *Golden Crown* and played a Goldfields side. The Auckland Football Club was formed in July 1870 and two more games of football were played against HMS *Rosario*. Altogether a busy year for Auckland football, and rugby was not far away.

In Wellington in 1868, a football game that was to have been played between the 18th Royal Irish Regiment and civilians failed to take place when insufficient civilians turned up. Instead, it was reported that a spirited game between two companies of the 18th Royal Irish was played near the Mount Cook barracks. In 1870 a one-off game of hybrid football was played between the visiting HMS *Rosario* and a Wellington team. This was followed by the first rugby game against the Nelson Rugby Football Club later the same year, but no club organisation immediately resulted from the game. It wasn't until 1871 that the Wellington Rugby Club, the second rugby club in New Zealand, was formed.

During May 1869 a couple of hybrid football games got a mention in the Dunedin press, with the comment: 'What sort of football they were playing, I doubt even the players knew.' A short-lived club was established and the press commented: 'If the club continues to exist . . . the committee will no doubt see the necessity of enforcing the rules adopted by the Melbourne Football Club.'

In 1871 George Sale, an old Rugbeian, together with George Thomson, organised a game based on Rugby School rules between teams from Otago University and Dunedin High School (renamed Otago Boys' High School in 1888). The game was played on 9 September 1871, on the Dunedin Oval, the first game of rugby to be played in Otago. On 12 March 1872, the Dunedin Football Club was formed under the guidance of Sale and Thomson. However, the club elected to draft its own compromise set of rules in order to appease all factions. In Dunedin, as in Christchurch, rugby struggled to gain acceptance and apart from the odd game played under rugby rules, it wasn't until 1877, when Dunedin clubs toured New Zealand, that the Dunedin club finally adopted the rugby game.

The Albert Barracks, Auckland, scene of some early games of hybrid football, home of the Auckland College and Grammar School for some years.

During the late 1860s and early 1870s, games of hybrid football were occurring infrequently in different locations. Victorian rules, soccer and rugby were part of the combinations played, and apart from Christ's College and the Christchurch Football Club, there was no commonality of rules and virtually no two games of football were the same. With communication between different settlements so difficult, people had no idea what was going on in other places. The only regular shipping connections were with Melbourne, Australia. All this was about to change. Rugby was about to happen.

In England, early football led to the development of two major codes. In New Zealand, without exception early football in its different forms merged into the game of rugby. Although hybrid games of football continued to be played sporadically in a few areas after 1870, its days were numbered.

Oft in the stilly night . . .
Fond memory brings the light
Of other days around me
The smiles, the tears, of boyhood years
The eyes that shone, Now dimm'd and gone

Thomas Moore

The Christ's College Game

THE CHRIST'S COLLEGE game of football was unique in New Zealand. Just as the Rugby School game of Bigside football was controlled by the pupils through the levee system, so the Christ's College game was administered and controlled by the pupils through the Games Committee. This included finances, ground maintenance, the provision of equipment, selections and the rules of the game. In 1862 the Games Committee, under the chairmanship of George Harper, appointed four boys to frame rules for the 'Game of Football'. The rules, known simply as the 'College Rules', were based loosely on the game that had been played at Radley College, England by Harper, and were largely consistent with a primitive version of soccer, although some handling was permitted.

The College Rules of 1862 were the first code of home-grown football rules of any sort to appear in New Zealand. The game was played on a pitch 150 yards by 76 yards, with an unlimited number of players, except in public matches, when each side was restricted to twenty-two players. Goals could be scored when the ball was 'fairly kicked or thrown into the goal'. Hacking was expressly forbidden. A further rule was soon added: 'That no tussock throwing be allowed during games of football', a reference to the condition of the grounds and to possible spectator practices during matches.

In the years that followed, Christ's College continued to play in-school games and at one stage it was compulsory for all boys selected to attend games. One unique feature was the recognition of the 'Twenty-two of Football', a practice that required formal Games Committee approval for any changes — the same as for the 'Eleven of Cricket'. The 'Twenty-two of Football' played the outside or 'Grand' games, although some fifteen-a-side games were played as well.

Committee meeting held in the Library Tuesday April 15th.
Present. All The members Except, Buttan, T Ollivier –
George Harper was Elected Chairman & Secretary
Henry Dudley was Elected Treasurer
Alfred Thompson & F Baker were proposed as
auditors, The Former Gentleman was Elected
He was also Elected vice–chairman.
H. Dudley moved & G. Harper Seconded
   "That there be one General fund for the
   School games."
After Some discussion this Motion was Carried
Nem Con –
George Harper, moved & H Dudley seconded.
   That a Select Committee of Persons be balloted
   for, to draw up a set of rules for the
   Guidance of the Committee –
Report to be brought up by the next meeting
   Messrs Thompson, Dudley, F Ollivier & Harper
   were Elected –
G. Harper moved & A Thompson sec d
   That a Select Committee of 4 Persons be balloted
   for to frame rules for the game of Football
   The Same Committee was Elected –

First minutes of the Games Committee, Christ's College, 1853.
Christ's College Archives, Games Committee Minute Book, 1853

In 1869 the Games Committee opened a subscription list to assist in defraying the expenses in levelling 'a piece of the paddock for a football ground' and sowing it with grass seed. The same year a challenge for a match was received from the 'High School' (not the present Christchurch Boys' High School, but a school of Presbyterian association). After agreeing on the rules, the first game of secondary school hybrid football in New Zealand was played at Hagley Park on 5 August 1869. Christ's College won by six goals to nil. In 1872, all Christ's College football teams were reduced to fifteen-a-side.

From the early days of Croasdaile Bowen, before the Games Committee was even established, Christ's College had been well aware of the rugby game, but had gone its own separate way. It remained staunch and true to its own tradition for almost twenty years, apart from occasional departures to play opponents' rules for outside games. Finally, in 1881, in the face of the obvious dominance of rugby, it abandoned its own version of football and embraced the rugby game. The Christ's College game, the first recognised game of structured football played in New Zealand, survived the longest of all the home-grown games and was the last to be abandoned in favour of rugby.

Chapter Six

The Father of New Zealand Rugby

ONE OF the leading contributors to the development of the New Zealand way of life was not an important politician, or an outstanding social reformer, but rather a mere nineteen-year-old youth who, because of his background and English education, might have been regarded as a bit of a toff. It all happened quickly, without any great ceremony, and then the momentum took over. The great saga began and the young man stepped back into relative obscurity and, as is so often the case, received little or no recognition.

Charles John Monro, the father of New Zealand rugby, is one of New Zealand's most unrecognised achievers. He was the son of Sir David Monro, Doctor of Medicine and pioneer settler, who arrived in Nelson in 1842, the first year of the settlement. Sir David was a magistrate and a local and national politician. He was one of the founding governors of Nelson College — Monro House at Nelson College was named after him. He rose to become Speaker of the House of Representatives in 1861 and was knighted in 1866.

Sir David Monro, a leading New Zealand pioneer statesman.
Nelson Provincial Museum, Tyree Studio Collection, 67894/3

Charles Monro was born at Waimea West, Nelson, on 5 April 1851. At the age of nine he followed his two older brothers, David, who had been a foundation pupil, and Alexander, and entered Nelson College in the preparatory department, probably as a boarder, where he remained until 1865. There are no surviving records of his time spent at college.

On his sixteenth birthday, Monro set out for England, with the intention of preparing for an army career. On 7 September 1867, he presented himself at Christ's College, Finchley, London. Christ's College was a private boarding school with a roll of 150 boys. Nineteenth-century English schools were not known for their home comforts and Christ's College was described by one boarder as a 'building of mid-Victorian gloom. The buildings were as cold as ice . . . and the gratings emitted . . . a most sickening odour.'

Christ's College, Finchley, was at the time only eleven years old and rugby was the accepted game. There young Monro was initiated into the rugby football game that he was to bring back with him to his homeland. The college historian recorded that Charles Monro played in the Second XX, that he won the school pole vault and that he was appointed as a sub-prefect in Extra Form II. Notwithstanding, he did not enjoy the spartan conditions at the school and he left in July 1869. He later confided to his children that he was only just able to bear it.

Apparently, Monro was not considered robust enough to go into the army and he returned to New Zealand, arriving in Nelson on the

Christ's College, Finchley, England, as it looked in Monro's time.
New Zealand Rugby Museum

Charles Monro, 'The Father of New Zealand Rugby',
aged twenty-three years.
Nelson Provincial Museum, Brown Collection, 11927/2

trans-Tasman trader *Airedale* on 27 January 1870. Monro's increased maturity impressed his illustrious father, who commented: 'Charlie seems to have been a general favourite at Home. He has grown a good deal, and is a nice, frank, gentleman-like boy.'

The advent of the Nelson Football Club during his absence overseas gave Monro the opportunity to suggest to the club that they try the game of rugby under his tuition, to which the club readily agreed. A similar proposal must have been made to Nelson College, then under the headmastership of Rev. Frank Simmons, himself an old Rugbeian, and Nelson College also elected to try the new game. After both teams had had practices under Monro's direction, a match was arranged. This match, the first rugby game in New Zealand, was played on 14 May 1870.

Monro played in this first game and continued to play for the Nelson Rugby Football Club and for combined Nelson clubs until 1875. He was a club committee member in 1870 and the club coach from 1870 to 1873. After 1875, there is no further mention made of him in rugby circles and he completely fades from the rugby scene.

He apparently worked for some time at Bankhouse, the large family-run holding at Renwick, near Blenheim, managed by his brother, Alexander. In 1882 he is recorded as being a freehold landowner of small holdings in Nelson, Picton, Wellington and Marton. On 17 March 1885, he married Helen Beatrice McDonald at Nelson Cathedral and they raised a family of three sons and two daughters.

In 1887 Monro moved to Palmerston North to take up 50 acres of land on top of the Fitzherbert West Hills overlooking the Manawatu Plains, and established a farm he called Craiglockhart. Like his father, Monro prospered and became a man of independent means, through farming, timber milling and flax milling. He introduced the Japanese plum into New Zealand.

In 1895, he helped found the first golf club in the area, the championship course at Hokowhitu, where he was the first club captain and president. The seventh hole at Hokowhitu is known as 'Monro's'. He was a good boxer and a fine horseman, having played in the first game of polo in New Zealand, at Nelson in 1871. He was much

Charles Monro, pictured about 1886 with his wife and oldest son David.
New Zealand Rugby Museum

sought-after as a fine baritone singer in local operatic shows because of his ability to sing arias in Italian, a talent he developed while spending nine months in Italy studying opera. He was also recognised as an authority on river protection and erosion control measures.

Monro had little to do with rugby in his later years and was largely quiet about his pioneering role. He seldom attended matches, although he did travel to Wellington in 1930 at the age of seventy-nine for the fourth test between New Zealand and the British Isles Lions, as the guest of the New Zealand Rugby Union. Monro died at Palmerston North on 9 April 1933. He is buried in the Kelvin Grove Cemetery, Palmerston North.

Throughout his life, Monro sought no praise or recognition for his achievements. He has never been honoured or recognised by any rugby organisation for his contribution to the game in New Zealand. Only on one occasion did Monro offer any public pronouncement on rugby. This was prompted when *The Dominion* newspaper carried an interview with one of his early Nelson team-mates, Robert Tennent, in 1928. As well as recording a couple of incorrect dates, *The Dominion* incorrectly described Tennent as the founder of New Zealand rugby. The error was *The Dominion*'s and not of Tennent's suggestion, although Monro did not appear to notice the distinction. In a letter to the editor published in *The Dominion* of 5 July 1928, he stated:

> I have known Mr Tennent for more than 60 years and when we were young I knew him extremely well, upon the football field and in many other relations. He has always been a man of great energy and credit is due to him for the enthusiasm with which he entered into all forms of athletic sports. But when he states that he was the founder of rugby football in New Zealand he is not correct . . .
>
> Mr Tennent was a member of the Nelson Football Club, not one of whom had ever seen the rugby game, which they adopted at my instigation and played under my tutelage until familiar with the rules. No credit is due to me in the matter; my introduction of rugby to my native land was merely a coincidence — a coincidence of circumstances. As a matter of fact, the first match at Petone was played in the same year that I introduced the game to Nelson. I made the whole arrangements, even to picking the Wellington team, since there was no football club there in those early days. It was Mr Tennent who wrote me asking if it could be possible to arrange the match, and he played as one of the Nelson team . . . I am not disposed to sit quietly down and allow my claim to be jumped by an old friend.

Although misdirected, Monro's rebuttal provides an interesting insight into the beginnings of rugby in Nelson and Wellington.

His grandson, Peter Gaisford, of Opotiki, remembers Monro well, having been raised in the large house at Craiglockhart from an early age: 'He was patriarchal but affectionate and a dead shot with a stone if he caught anyone poaching his garden. He was also mildly eccentric, having once imported Chinese firecrackers to insert in the frames of hanging pictures as an early form of fire alarm, the theory being that the explosions would wake or alert the household to the danger before the house was consumed in flames. He never spoke much of his status as the father of New Zealand rugby. I think we were more proud of him for being the father of rugby than he was, and more glory was reflected on us than he ever claimed for himself.'

Craiglockhart. Named after the Monro country estate in Scotland.
New Zealand Rugby Museum

Charles Monro was New Zealand-born. His achievement is remarkable when viewed in the context of the time. New Zealand had been a self-governing colony for only fourteen years since 1856 and was still being pioneered and governed by Englishmen, born in England. One of the early European children born in this country, Monro was arguably the first native-born New Zealander to ascend the stairway of achievement. His legacy was both unparalleled and far reaching. He remains all but forgotten.

Often I think of the beautiful town

That is seated by the sea

Often in thought go up and down

The pleasant streets of that dear old town

And my youth comes back to me . . .

It murmurs and whispers still

A boy's will is the wind's will

And the thoughts of youth are long, long thoughts.

Longfellow

Charles Monro, aged seventy-nine years.
Nelson Provincial Museum, Cooper-Sharp Collection, 223693/9

Chapter Seven
1870 — the First Rugby Match

THE FIRST settlers arrived in Nelson in February 1842, and within six months the township had a population of about 2000. Nelson College opened in 1856, in temporary premises on Catholic Hill in Manuka Street. In 1861 the college shifted from its temporary premises to its present site in Waimea Road. The magnificent new wooden building was designed by notable architect William Beatson as a miniature replica of Eton College. It was described at the time as the largest building in the colony and the premier school.

The first recognised rugby match in New Zealand, organised by Charles Monro on his return from England, was played at the Botanics Reserve, Nelson between the Nelson Football Club and Nelson College, on Saturday, 14 May 1870.

It wasn't until 1963, more than ninety years later, after extensive investigation by New Zealand Rugby Football Union historian Arthur Swan, that the New Zealand union formally recognised this game as the first rugby match played in New Zealand, and the Nelson club as New Zealand's first rugby club. Swan spent years scouring the columns of old newspapers in order to establish how and when rugby began in different parts of New Zealand. His task was made considerably more difficult because most players in those early years would not have known which rules or version they were playing, much less the ignorance of the reporters sent along to write about these 'football' matches.

Trafalgar Street, Nelson, circa 1870.
Nelson Provincial Museum, Copy Collection, C3106

In 1870 the small, isolated settlement of Nelson was still less than thirty years old and had a population of 5530. Sports competition as we understand it today was scarce. There was a regatta club, a gymnasium club and a summer cricket competition with about five regular teams, but there were no regular winter sports, other than the occasional hybrid football match.

A game of football was probably quite an event in the small community and would have been anticipated with some enthusiasm and interest. The players who took part in the first rugby match probably comprised a good number of the keen, active young men of the town. With little knowledge of the rules or skills of the game, they looked forward to the prospect of a rugged physical encounter and a team contest. There were eighteen players in each team, the college team having been picked from a total school roll of sixty-one. The names of the teams are not recorded, although by examining newspaper records and other archives of the period, it is possible to ascertain the names of most of the likely players who took part in this historic game.

Botanics Reserve, Nelson, circa 1870.
Nelson Provincial Museum, Bett Collection, 1/4 142

It is probable that the Nelson College team included such notables as F.B. Wither, Charles Pratt, J. Burnett, C.R. Vickerman, E.F. Blundell, J.R.B. Roy, G.A. Nicholson, W.H. Barnicoat, A.B. Campbell, J. Warnock, J.W. Blackett, W.E. Clouston and J.G. Blackett. Similarly, it can be deduced that the Nelson club side probably included Charles Monro, Alfred Drew, Robert Tennent, W.G. Tennent, J. Clark, H.E.P. Adams, A.S. Otterson, H. Blundell, C.S. Cross, T.A. Nicholson, W.G. Nicholson, G.F. Butt, J.H. Williamson and A. Kilgour. The *Nelson Examiner* noted that the College team looked very well in their tight-fitting shirts and blue caps (they probably wore their gymnasium attire, including white knickerbockers) and that the Nelson club, having no distinctive uniform, did not look as well as their opponents (they wore their street clothes). Nelson club won by two goals to nil.

The fact the teams were eighteen-a-side was a matter of agreement between the captains and was in keeping with some of the formations of those early days; '10 forwards, three halfbacks, three three-quarters and two fullbacks (goal minders)'. College won the toss and elected to kick off, the game commencing soon after 2 p.m.

An account of the game is given in the Nelson *Colonist* of Tuesday, 17 May 1870:

FOOTBALL MATCH, THE COLLEGE v TOWN.

An enthusiastic football player sends us the following account of this game: The toss for the 'kick off' being won by the College, the respective sides are placed by the captains. First the 'kick off', with the fast runners in attendance to follow up the ball; next, a few to back them up, the 'long kicks' in the rear, and then the 'goal minders'. The other side stand well back to catch the ball for a run, or long kick, to get it back past the 'kick off', with a few to charge the foremost of their opponents.

And now, what was comparative silence and inactivity, is suddenly converted into a rushing, noisy, shouting crew, and as the ball is kicked off the game commences in earnest. Almost as soon as the ball is amongst the Town players, the College have followed up, when a kick sends it over their heads again, and then it is seen in one place, and then in another, the whole field in pursuit. Now some player runs with it, and a general scrimmage ensures; it is all shove, pull, rush and roll about in a confused mass till 'down' is cried, and away the ball goes again till perchance it gets in touch or caught.

At first the College had it all their own way, and seemed intent on rushing the goal before the Town players shook themselves together; the ball was repeatedly charged close up to the goal, but was always got rid of safely. Now the Town side began to play better, and by taking advantage of a chance, runs right down to the College goal, and the ball is 'touched down' behind the goal, and when kicked out before the College can charge him, Drew has kicked a splendid goal, for the Town, after a long and obstinately contested game.

After a short respite the goals are changed, and the game resumed. Again the silence is broken . . . with yells of 'off side', 'touch it down', etc; again the whole field seems in a rapid move, in first one and then another direction, or engaged in a scrimmage, or a long run, or waiting eagerly for the ball to be thrown in from 'touch', while some unfortunate may be seen hopping temporarily to the rear to repair damages.

Presently the ball is kicked through the College goal by Clark, and so the game terminates in favour of the Town Club.

The *Examiner* of Wednesday, 18 May 1870, also contained a report of the match, commenting: 'College played well and made a hard fight of it, determined not to give up, but at last a sudden rush by Monro and Clark decided the matter, the latter managing to kick a goal. About 200 spectators assembled to witness the game and seemed to enjoy it as much as the players themselves, laughing heartily at the various spills, etc.'

Charles Monro's parents were among the spectators. The day was described as being 'very favourable, rather cloudy and quite calm, and the field was decorated with a fair sprinkling of ladies and a goodly number of the opposite sex [sic], who seemed to enjoy the changeful fortunes of the game.' The *Nelson Examiner* reported that the game had not been expected to finish that afternoon, 'but so it happened and there being several fresh onlookers anxious to play, a fresh game was started and continued until all had had enough of football for one afternoon'.

Neither of the local papers seemed to grasp the significance of the occasion. *The Colonist* described the game as a 'Football Match' and the *Nelson Examiner* referred to the game as 'the first football match of the season'. Neither paper makes mention of the fact that it was a rugby match, let alone that it was the first rugby match played in Nelson or, for that matter, New Zealand. A historic event went unsung and largely unnoticed. There were probably other games of football played elsewhere in the country on the same day. In particular a scratch game of hybrid football was played by members of the Christchurch Football Club at Latimer Square in Christchurch, but Nelson was the only place where rugby was played.

The next game of the 1870 season in Nelson was between Sixteen Old College Members of the club and Sixteen Who Were Not Collegians. The match was played on one Saturday and

A 1991 re-enactment of the first rugby match by Nelson College students. Note the caps and goalposts.
Nelson Mail

then, because the rules required matches to continue until one side had scored two goals, an abandonment was agreed upon after several wet Saturdays. Two matches between sides alphabetically chosen, A to K versus L to Z and then A to H versus I to Z, were played next, with Nelson club and Nelson College players being in the selections.

The final match of the season was played in Wellington on 12 September, between a Wellington side, organised and coached by Charles Monro while visiting Wellington, and the Nelson Rugby Football Club. Nelson College's role was significant in that twelve of the players were old collegians — ten played for Nelson and two for Wellington. Monro was thus responsible for introducing rugby to Wellington as well as Nelson. Many years later Monro recorded that these games had been played with rugby balls. It is believed that he brought four oval balls with him into New Zealand when he returned from England.

The 1871 *Nelson Almanac*, in summarising the important events of 1870, records seven entries for May, but makes no mention of the first rugby game, although the 12 September fixture against Wellington was considered worthy of inclusion.

The Botanics Reserve as it is today, with commemorative stone cairn erected by the Nelson Rugby Football Club.

The other notable event that occurred in 1870 was the announcement by the Colonial Treasurer, Julius Vogel, to an astonished House that the government was to borrow 10 million pounds to finance a public works programme. This policy was to have considerable impact on the growth and development of rugby over the next thirty years.

After Nelson and Wellington, rugby began to be introduced in other areas, particularly Wanganui, Auckland, Thames and Taranaki, mainly by expatriate English public school old pupils.

This they all with joyful mind
Bear through life like a torch in flame,
And falling fling to the host behind —
'Play up! Play up! And play the game!'

Henry Newbolt

81

Chapter Eight

All Go in Nelson and Wellington

Wᴇ ɴᴏᴡ ʟᴏᴏᴋ at the events that followed the establishment of New Zealand's first rugby club, the Nelson Rugby Football Club. For many years this distinction had been claimed by the Christchurch Football Club, which was undoubtedly New Zealand's first football club, but not the first rugby football club. It was owing to the initiative of Robert Tennent, only recently shifted to Nelson, that the Nelson Football Club was formed in 1868. When the club was reconstituted as the Nelson Rugby Football Club in 1870, Tennent became the first secretary-treasurer, Alfred Drew chairman-club captain, Charles Monro coach, Henry Adams, Henry Blundell and Alfred Otterson the committee members.

The events leading to the first outside game, in 1870, against a Wellington team are significant and worth relating. As recorded by *The Dominion*, Tennent had written to Monro, who was staying in Wellington with his father during the parliamentary session, requesting that he arrange a match with the capital city. Unfortunately, there was no Wellington team in existence, so Monro took it upon himself to arrange and coach a team and to organise the match.

Organising a Wellington team was easier said than done, as in spite of previous efforts, there was no football organisation of any kind in Wellington at that time. However, after ten days he was able to report to Nelson that he had gathered together a team, including members of the local armed constabulary. What a team it was! With the exception of two or three recent arrivals from Britain, none of the players had even seen a rugby ball, but as Monro commented: 'They were all willing to put up a fight, if we would give them a few preliminary lessons in the game.'

The next problem was how to get the Nelson men over to Wellington — there was no regular inter-island service at that time. Using his father's connections, Monro approached Julius Vogel, in his capacity as Minister of Marine, and asked him if the government steamer *Luna*, which was on a lighthouse supply run to the Marlborough Sounds, Golden Bay and Tasman Bay, could transport the players. Vogel kindly agreed and telegraphed Captain Fairchild, instructing him to call at Nelson and bring the team to Wellington.

Finding a suitable playing venue also presented difficulties. Wellington's only place for recreation of this kind was the Basin Reserve, which had been Wellington's cricket ground since 1866, but it was badly waterlogged at the time. Monro related: 'There was a vacant section off Hobson Street and an area at Te Aro popularly known as Johnny Martin's Paddock. Inspection proved both of these to be too small so I walked out to the Hutt in the search for a playing field, and got permission from Mr Alfred Lumsden to set up our goal-posts in one of his paddocks, and then footed it back to town.

'When the Nelson club team arrived, they were given a day or two to recuperate after their voyage, and the next day the two teams were driven out to the Hutt in a couple of Prosser's flat-deck drays. A good deal of rain had fallen in the last few days and Mr Lumsden's paddock was found to be too wet. We drove back to Petone

The government steamship *Luna*, which took the first Nelson club side to Wellington in 1870.
Alexander Turnbull Library, Wellington, De Mans Collection, G-14954-1/2

with our impedimenta and there, on a dry and stony place close to where the railway station now stands, we set up our goal-posts.'

What energy was expended and hardship endured to play this historic game of rugby on 12 September 1870. It was the first rugby game to be played in Wellington. The Nelson club fielded fourteen players, including Monro, but the Wellington side could muster only twelve. However, the dray driver, Stan Prosser, was persuaded to play for Wellington, taking their number to thirteen. The result, as was to be expected, was a win to the Nelson club, the score being two goals to one. Cross and Drew scored Nelson's goals.

Arthur Swan recorded the teams as follows:

Nelson clubs: A Drew (captain), H.E.P. Adams, R.C. Tennent, G.F. Butt, C.J. Monro, H. Blundell, Hill, Barnes, J.H. Williamson, A.S. Otterson, C.S. Cross, W.G. Nicholson, T.H. Nicholson, J. Clark. *Wellingtonians*: J.C.R. Isherwood (captain), F.M. Oliver, J. Beetham, R.G. Park, C. Nation, A.M. Beale, Hon. Hussey Vivian, T. Hoggard, Crampton, H.H. Travers, A.R. Baker, J. MacAra, S. Prosser.

Monro played an extraordinary part in the game. He played for his home side, was opposition selector and coach, and refereed the game as well. He later wrote: 'There was no referee with his confounded whistle to check almost every heroic effort, but Lord how we did enjoy ourselves, and how little did we think that we were the pioneers of New Zealand's great national game.'

The *Wellington Independent* reported:

> The first goal was gained by the Nelson men after a hard tussle; the next by the Wellingtonians after a still longer contest. The following one was scored to the Nelson side; but as so often happens in this game, different codes of law prevailed in the minds of the players, but without for an instant promoting ill-feeling . . . so that the Nelson men carried the day. Their players had the evident advantage of belonging to a club and of having played together often, whereas the Wellington men met as so many strangers.

This situation was not to endure in Wellington for long, because the Wellington Football Club was formed on 12 May 1871. A combined Nelson clubs side, comprising ten from the Nelson club and four from Nelson College, played the newly formed Wellington club in a fourteen-a-side match at the Basin Reserve on 29 September. The match was played before a crowd of 400 spectators, including the Governor, Sir George Bowen, and Lady Bowen, who watched from their carriage. Wellington won a robust contest by one goal to nil. This was the first inter-provincial club match played in New Zealand.

The outstanding feature seems to have been the after-match dinner held at the Empire Hotel. The dinner was apparently excellent and was followed by the most extensive list of toasts, with musical honours, that could be thought of. These included the Nelson and Wellington football clubs, the army, the navy, and the armed constabulary, Sir George and Lady Bowen, the House of Representatives, the press of the colony and many others. Most of the toasts were replied to and, it was reported, 'the most genial and kindly feeling was manifested and the small hours arrived before the company broke up'.

The 1872 season was important for being the first occasion an outside match was played in Nelson. The Wellington club arrived to play a fourteen-a-side game. Because of inclement weather on the morning of the match, the captains agreed to postpone the match for a day. The Wellington team quickly settled down to enjoy the conviviality and pleasures of the local hostelry: a sumptuous meal, followed by some steady imbibing. However, their surfeiting was interrupted when Nelson club officials emerged through the pipe smoke to inform them that the rain had stopped and request that the game proceed. Arrangements had been made for banks, offices and ships to close for the match and if the game wasn't played that day, it would not be possible for many of the players to get time off the following day.

The Wellington players somewhat reluctantly agreed to play, apart from one individual who adamantly refused to do so, and the match took place as scheduled in sodden conditions on 11 June 1872. Not surprisingly, Combined Nelson Clubs won by three goals to nil. Wellington's problems did not end there. The non-arrival of the steamer delayed the team's departure for several days, during which time a further fifteen-a-side game was played. The bad weather

The 1873 Nelson Club team, probably the oldest rugby photograph in New Zealand. Note the team caps.
Nelson Provincial Museum, Cooper-Sharp Collection, 223696/9

continued and when the Wellington team finally departed, a southerly gale in Cook Strait forced the steamer to turn back and take shelter in Bowden's Bay, near Tory Channel, for two days. The entire trip lasted ten days instead of the anticipated four.

In 1873 a combined Nelson clubs side journeyed to Wellington, where a drawn match was played on 15 August before a large crowd that included the new Governor, Sir James Fergusson. The *Nelson Examiner* commented on the team uniforms: 'Each side, of course had its uniform — the Nelsonians, white singlets and knickerbockers, with magenta stockings and black cap; the Wellingtonians, white singlets, blue serge knickerbockers, light grey stocking and blue cap.' At this stage it was quite common for players to wear their caps during a game. Nelson's home season included games between Lightweights and Heavyweights, and between Country Aristocrats and Town Bumpkins.

There was no match against Wellington in 1874, because of a decline of support for the game in the capital. However, there was compensation when the combined Nelson clubs played a match against a visiting British warship, HMS *Blanche*. The Nelson club also played a match against the Artillery Cadet Corps and later there was a Lawyers and Town versus Country game.

In 1875 Nelson hosted two visiting teams, a Wellington Club side on 5 July and Auckland Provincial Clubs on 27 September, as part of Auckland's historic tour. Local games between composite or invited teams were again played during the season and this continued to be the typical playing format for several years to come.

By the end of 1875, all of the six founding committee members of the Nelson Rugby Football Club had left Nelson. We have already looked at the life of Charles Monro, and it is appropriate to also examine the lives of two of the other founding members of the club, both of whom were outstanding contributors to the establishment of pioneer rugby in New Zealand.

The founder of the Nelson Rugby Football Club, Robert Tennent, continued to follow a banking career with the Bank of New South Wales. On New Year's Day, 1872, he won what was described as the inaugural New Zealand one-mile athletics title. From Nelson he moved to open a new branch at Patea, where he helped to establish the Patea Rugby Football Club in 1876. He subsequently managed branches in Wanganui, Wellington, Auckland, Blenheim, Dunedin, Timaru and finally Invercargill, from where he retired at the age of seventy.

He played tennis, golf and later bowls, and was for some years treasurer of the Timaru and Invercargill golf clubs. He helped to establish the present Timaru links and the Otatara links in Invercargill. He died on 14 April 1939, a few weeks short of his ninetieth birthday. Tennent was buried in a small cemetery just north of the Manawatu Gorge, near Woodville. In 1970, at the centenary of the Nelson Rugby Football Club, the Bank of New South Wales presented the R.C. Tennent Cup to the club, the only known recognition given to any of the three founding fathers of New Zealand rugby.

Robert Collings Tennent, a pioneer sporting visionary, and his wife.
Nelson Provincial Museum, Isaacs & Clark Collection, 844

Alfred Drew, the first club captain of the Nelson Rugby Football Club, was a contemporary of Monro at Nelson College. He shifted from Nelson in 1871 and established rugby in Wanganui the following year. The first game, Town versus Country, was played at Aramaho. Drew, a watchmaker by trade, then moved to New Plymouth, where he helped to establish the Taranaki Rugby Football Club in 1874 and was the first club captain. He continued his involvement and completed a great lifetime contribution to the game, as a referee in Manawatu.

A man of many parts, Drew was conductor of the Palmerston North choral society for many years, organist at the local All Saints Church, and a member of the Masonic Lodge. He was a foundation member of the Palmerston North Bowling Club, and won a North Island singles bowls title. One of the movers and shapers of early New Zealand rugby, Alfred Drew played rugby in four different districts and played a key role in establishing three of New Zealand's pioneer rugby clubs. He died at Sanson, Manawatu, on 13 February 1925.

It is interesting to note that the three leading figures in the establishment of the Nelson Rugby Football Club — Monro, Tennent and Drew — all lie buried within 50 kilometres of each other in the Manawatu.

Alfred Drew, 'The Club Maker'.
Nelson Provincial Museum, Davis Collection, 529/1

The goodliest fellowship of famous knights
Whereof this world holds record . . .
I think that we shall never more at any future time
Delight our souls with talk of knightly deeds
As in the days that were.

Lord Tennyson

New Zealand Rugby — Timeline

Pre Rugby

1854   First recorded game of informal football in New Zealand played in Christchurch.

1860   A game of primitive rugby is played by students at Nelson College.

1862   Christ's College begins playing its own version of football.

1863   The Christchurch Football Club is formed.

Rugby Period

1870   The first rugby match in New Zealand is played at Nelson. The first rugby club, the Nelson Rugby Football Club, is formed.

1871   The Wellington Rugby Football Club is formed.

1874   Four new rugby clubs formed in Auckland. Auckland interclub competition begins.

1875   Auckland Provincial Clubs tour New Zealand. First recognised inter-provincial match played between Auckland and Otago.

1876   First secondary school match played between Nelson College and Wellington College.

1879   First New Zealand provincial union, the Canterbury Rugby Football Union, is formed, followed by Wellington later the same year.

1882   First overseas team, New South Wales, tours New Zealand.

1884   First New Zealand team tours New South Wales. Use of whistles by referees introduced.

1887   First New Zealand captain, William Millton, dies of typhoid, aged 27.

1888   Visit to New Zealand by Andrew Stoddart's British team.

1888–89 New Zealand Native team tours Australia and Britain.

1889   First sevens rugby played, in Dunedin.

1892   New Zealand Rugby Football Union founded.

1893   First New Zealand team selected under the auspices of the New Zealand Rugby Football Union tours Australia.

1894   First match played by New Zealand in New Zealand — against New South Wales.

1895   Auckland inter-secondary schools rugby competition established.

1896   First conference of New Zealand Rugby Referees Association held.

1897   First North Island versus South Island match played at Wellington.

1902   Ranfurly Shield presented to the New Zealand Rugby Football Union by Lord Ranfurly.

Chapter Nine

The Game Takes Root

RUGBY WAS a public school game created by and for the offspring of the English middle classes, which was eagerly embraced in a far-flung colony settled largely by the downstairs classes. There can be no doubt that rugby suited the lifestyles and landscapes of early New Zealand. The enthusiasm with which rugby was accepted leaves no doubt that a situation existed that was simply waiting for the right game to eventuate. Rugby was obviously that game.

With the advent of rugby in Nelson and Wellington in 1870, the seeds of New Zealand rugby were sown. New Zealand in 1870 was a land of small and scattered settlements, most affected to some degree by the gold rushes in the south or by the now-called New Zealand wars in the north. The total population, excluding Maori, was 256,000.

The Wellington Football Club was formally established in 1871. On 11 May, the following advertisement appeared in the *Daily Advertiser*: 'We remind all our sporting friends that a meeting of gentlemen interested in football, paper hunts and other good old English sports, will be held at the Branch Hotel tomorrow evening.' About thirty people were present at the 12 May meeting, which had been preceded by a paper chase through the streets of Wellington. The resolution to form a club was unanimously adopted and Captain J.C.R. Isherwood was elected as the first club president.

The Wellington club played Victorian football for the first part of the season, but adopted rugby rules from 1 July. At first some difficulty was experienced. There was some discontent among the players, particularly from those new to the game and to the rugby rules. The *Evening Post* recorded: 'A little rough work was tried by some who appeared willing at least to bring the rugby rules into discredit, but in spite of this we think that when they are better known they will be well liked.' These last words proved prophetic, as the initial antipathy soon settled. The club recorded three games in its first season, two against the Armed Constabulary and one against combined Nelson clubs at the Basin Reserve on 29 September.

The early years of the Wellington club were not without their setbacks, particularly in 1874 and 1875, when unsuccessful attempts were made to establish Victorian rules clubs in Wellington. The Wellington rugby club reached a low point, and problems were experienced in fielding a team. A letter published in the *Evening Post* of 3 August 1874 illustrated the difficulties the club faced:

> Sir, Could you, or any of your numerous readers, inform me, as well as a few others 'who would like to know, you know,' under what recognized rules (if any) the local football club play? I am etc COUSIN JACK.

A reply was published in the *Evening Post* of 5 August:

> Sir, In answer to your correspondent, 'Cousin Jack', I beg to say that the rules laid down by the Wellington Football Club are identical with those of 'Rugby Union', which are the recognised rules of the twenty leading London football clubs, but unfortunately, on account of the apathy displayed by the youths of this city, who prefer the part of 'lookers on' to that of joining in the game, we can seldom raise full sides, which obliges us to curtail those rules to suit members. I am, etc TOUCH DOWN.

However, the setbacks were short-lived and the club was eventually able to consolidate and carve its own niche in New Zealand rugby history.

Another important development occurred in 1872, when rugby was introduced to Wanganui by Alfred Drew, who had been the first club captain of the Nelson club. The first game in Wanganui, a twenty-a-side match, was played on Walkers Paddock at Aramoho on 22 June between two sides assembled under the designations of Town and Country. The game, spread over two Saturdays, was finally abandoned without a result, after some strong tactics by one of the rustics caused the Town captain to indignantly lead his team off the field. Wirihana, who played for Country in the match, may well have been the first Maori to play in any organised game of rugby.

The formation of a club in Wanganui, the third rugby club in New Zealand, soon followed. This took place on 20 July, at a meeting in the Phoenix Hotel. Before the season ended, the club played two matches between composite sides drawn from its own members.

The Wellington team which visited Nelson in 1875, captain Isherwood fourth from left. The team included two players co-opted from a Victorian rules team.
New Zealand Rugby Museum

Auckland converted to rugby in 1873. The Auckland Football Club had been formed in 1870 and hybrid football had been played in the city and in the Thames area for three years, and a ten-a-side game had been played in 1872 between the Auckland club and Thames. There is strong evidence that the game was played according to rugby rules, which would make it the first game of rugby played in the Auckland area. However, the game was not recognised by Arthur Swan. This was probably because of the reduced number of players, but also because they had no rugby rules available to them at the time. The decision to adopt the rugby code was made at the Auckland club's annual meeting on 8 April 1873 at the initiative of C.B. Mercer, formerly of Wellington College, England, and C.G.R. Gore, formerly of the Wellington Football Club. The first games were based on the rules of the Wellington Football Club, as provided by Gore.

After a few practice runs, the first recognised rugby game in Auckland, a rather disorganised affair, was played on 3 May 1873, between Thirteen Colonials and Eight Outsiders. No goal was obtained by either side, but one touchdown was scored by the Colonials. The North Shore club began to function in the same year and the two clubs Auckland and North Shore, after an early scratch game, played their first interclub match, a twelve-a-side, on 26 July, when a drawn game was recorded. Further games were played in Auckland in 1873, including a ten-a-side match between the two combined Auckland clubs and the Thames club, which had also adopted the rugby version.

At the end of 1873 there were still only seven rugby clubs in New Zealand — Nelson, Nelson College, Wellington, Wanganui, Auckland, North Shore and Thames. In a few short years an explosion of clubs would take place.

Rugby began in Waikato in the following year, 1874, with a game between a team of locals calling themselves the Hamilton Bounders and a surveyors team called the Elephants. The term 'Bounders' was dropped when the Hamilton team later played a Cambridge team on 10 October. The Taranaki club began to function in 1874, owing largely to the efforts of the ubiquitous Alfred Drew, who had shifted from Wanganui to New Plymouth. The Egmont and Country clubs were also formed in Taranaki, but were short-lived, because most of their members were armed constabulary or garrison troops who were transferred on. This was part of the pattern of growth during the early years of rugby in New Zealand and was to be the fate of many of the clubs that were formed during this period.

Four new rugby clubs — Grafton, Parnell, Mount Hobson and Ponsonby — were formed in Auckland in 1874, bringing the total number of clubs in Auckland to six. During the year, the Auckland clubs began playing a somewhat stuttering interclub competition on Saturdays at Domain Hollow, North Shore and at the Metropolitan Ground. Auckland was on a roll. Not only were these the first regular club competition games organised in New Zealand, but also, probably in the world. They were the forerunner of the local club championships that were to be established throughout the country and would provide the platform for the growth of New Zealand rugby.

There is a strong suggestion that the Auckland Football Club, with many of its players dispersed to help establish other clubs, became the co-ordinating organisation for the early club competition and a social meeting place for the young men of substance in the town. The 1874 census records that the European population of Auckland, excluding North Shore, was 21,803, which made it the largest centre in New Zealand. Auckland, by virtue of its population, was playing a key role in establishing rugby in New Zealand.

In those early days the object of rugby was still to score goals. These could be gained from a place-kick, a drop-kick, or a kick off the ground from the field, known as a 'speculator', which counted as much as any other goal. Tries were desirable mainly because they gave the opportunity for a place-kick at goal. Games were won by the number of goals scored, but sometimes captains arranged for tries to count in the event of the score being equal or if no goals had been scored.

The captains interpreted the rules as the game proceeded. They had no guiding principle other than the knowledge of rugby verbally expounded by enthusiasts who had played the game in England. Even these enthusiasts differed at times, and matches were often held up while a point was debated. Soon umpires began to officiate and by 1873 printed rule books began to arrive in the country. This produced more consensus and cut down on the number

The Basin Reserve 1875, scene of early encounters between Wellington and visiting sides.

of disputes. By 1875, New Zealand had generally adopted fifteen-a-side and was ahead of the English union in this respect.

In 1875, the Dunedin club was joined by members of the Union club and played its first game of rugby against the touring Auckland Provincial Clubs team. Rugby arrived in Otago partly through the efforts of old Rugbeian, George Sale. He was born in Rugby, England in 1831, the son of a Rugby School teacher, and in 1845 had reputedly contributed to the writing of *The Laws of Football* at Rugby School.

The South Canterbury club of Timaru was established in April 1875, and this was followed a week later by the formation of the Temuka club. Both these clubs were formed through the efforts of Alfred St George Hamersley, who in 1873 had been captain of the English international side. The Christchurch Football Club played the South Canterbury club at rugby at Ashburton on Queen's Birthday, 1875, and formally converted to rugby from the beginning of the following season, after Montague Lewin successfully moved that the club adopt the Rugby Football Union rules.

Other clubs to form in 1875 were Napier, Blenheim, Greymouth and Hamilton. Even in isolated Greymouth rugby had taken root. Th*e Grey River Argus* reported on the opening of the season:

> There was an excellent muster and the ground was in fair order. Sides were chosen by Mr Newton and Mr Ahearn . . . Mr Ahearn's team scored two goals while their opponents did not get any. Mr North and Mr Warner then picked sides . . . The result was a goal to each side. The best of feeling was manifested throughout, everyone taking his 'spills' in good part.

At the end of 1875, the total number of rugby clubs stood at fifteen, with the Christchurch and Dunedin hybrid football clubs both flirting with rugby. It was not uncommon in those early years for a club to play one code of football one week and a different version the next, depending on their opponents.

The outstanding event of 1875 was the southern tour by the Auckland Provincial Clubs team, captained by G. Dunnett, the first team to tour New Zealand. Initially, twenty-five players from Auckland, Hamilton and Thames had been expected to tour, but defections cut the number to seventeen; one from Hamilton and the other sixteen from Auckland, and that included men who had earlier been regarded as back-up players. However, it was too late to make any fresh arrangements and despite difficulties until the last moment, the team left on one of the pluckiest ventures ever undertaken. It was an 1800-mile round trip and most of the time was spent at sea in uncomfortable conditions on board the small, coal-fired sailing steamer *Hawea*, which had been made available to the team by the recently formed Union Steamship Company.

The tour was exhausting, seasickness was rife and the demands placed on the players were excessive. With an average weight of just over 11 stone (70 kilograms), they were outweighed, outmuscled and outplayed by all their opponents. They played five matches within a fortnight, all of which were lost. All games were fifteen-a-side — the first to be played in New Zealand.

The team arrived in Wellington for their first match at 10 a.m. and, according to the 1888 *Auckland Football Annual*, played that same afternoon on a small ground against a very heavy team. The players did not recover from this match throughout the trip. The Wellington club team beat the Aucklanders 16–1.

Before the second match, in Dunedin, the team had a day's spell, the only break of the whole tour. The game against Otago clubs Dunedin and Union was played at the

The 1875 Auckland Provincial Clubs side which took rugby to New Zealand.

Recreation Ground Oval before an enthusiastic crowd of 3000, at that time the largest rugby crowd in the colony, and resulted in a 9½–1½ win to the locals. The big crowd can be partly attributed to the fact that Dunedin was the second largest city in the colony at the time, with a population of 18,500. This match is now recognised as the first inter-provincial rugby fixture played in New Zealand, because players in both teams were selected from different clubs (although three players from the Union club were accorded 'individual' status).

Then it was north to Christchurch for a game against the Christchurch club, whose players had assiduously practised rugby rules throughout August. Again the odds were stacked against the Aucklanders, who arrived in Christchurch at 11 a.m., just hours before their match. The match was played at Cranmer Square, also before 3000 spectators, and the home team won 9½–0.

The tourists then played a composite Nelson and Picton clubs team at Nelson and lost 6½–½. The fifth match was against Taranaki and, as usual, the players had no chance to give a good account of themselves. As soon as their vessel docked they disembarked and headed straight for the ground. Not surprisingly, they lost 9½–1.

Upon their return to Auckland, the tourists played an Auckland All Comers team and suffered a 21½–1½ defeat, their heaviest of the tour.

An artist's impression of an early New Zealand game. Note the upright stance of the players in the maul.
New Zealand Rugby Museum

Despite the hardships endured and losing every match, the epochal tour did more to establish the game of rugby in New Zealand than any other previous event. In particular, it was the means of establishing rugby in Otago and Canterbury. From a results standpoint, the tour was a failure, but in other respects it was a huge success. It established contacts between rugby-playing clubs in different parts of the country and fostered the idea that rugby was a countrywide movement. Through these contacts, ongoing relations were forged that were to be the basis for the inter-provincial rivalries to come.

A Canterbury Provincial Clubs side, made up of players drawn from Christchurch teams, made a curtailed three-match tour the following year and the Dunedin clubs made a similar six-match tour in 1877, albeit a much more successful one.

For when the great scorer comes
to mark against your name
He writes not that you won or lost
but how you played the game.

Grantland Rice

History of Scoring

In the earliest days of football at Rugby School, a match was won by the first side to obtain two goals. Initially, goals were scored by kicking the ball under the crossbar, then later over the crossbar. Scoring was very much a reflection of a side's ability to kick, usually by a drop-kick at goal from the field of play, or a free 'try' at goal after running in and touching the ball down over the opponents' goal line. The touchdown itself was valueless, regardless of whether the kick at goal was successful or not. Goals had no actual points value and the game was won simply by the number of goals scored unless pre-agreed otherwise.

As rugby spread, other methods of scoring gradually crept in: touchdowns in a team's own in-goal area, a try over the opponents' goal line and a scored goal. In the absence of goals, tries and touchdowns could count in the result. By 1875 there was general agreement that three touchdowns in own goal were equal to one try and three tries were the equivalent of one goal. Scoring methods were still often very ad hoc and varied from game to game and place to place.

Point values were introduced in 1886 as the first act of the International Rugby Board. In 1887 a try was generally valued at one point, but was still inferior to the goal, valued at three points. Point values still varied greatly until England joined the International Rugby Board in 1890 and uniform values were agreed and adopted.

Over the years point values have been modified and changed and today the try is worth a greater number of points than any form of kicked goal, while a touchdown in-goal is worth nothing.

Chapter Ten

Like Fire in the Pig Fern

I N ENGLAND, rugby had been established mainly around the English public school system. In New Zealand, the game was built largely upon an independent club system and the playing of regular weekly interclub competitions at a local level. Rugby in New Zealand was a game that transcended class distinctions. The butcher's boy would play and fraternise with the local doctor, the town youths would play with the local policeman, and secondary school pupils would play with their school masters. It was truly a classless game, very much suited to a largely egalitarian colonial society.

In 1876, six years after the first game was played in New Zealand, twenty further clubs were established, with Taranaki leading the way. The new Taranaki clubs were Pukearuke Armed Constabulary, Tikorangi and Beach School; in the southern area, the Patea club was established on the initiative of Robert Tennent, of Nelson club fame, and the Hawera-Waihi club was formed. Four new clubs were formed in Canterbury, three in Southland and three in Waikato. Other new clubs were Rangitikei, Marton, Oamaru and Wairarapa. The first inter-collegiate match was played (see Chapter 11).

During 1876, the Canterbury clubs decided to emulate their Auckland visitors of the previous season and dispatch a provincial side on a northern tour. The touring party, once again subject to last-minute withdrawals, consisted of eighteen players, drawn from four different Canterbury and South Canterbury clubs, including the Christchurch Football Club, which had changed to rugby that year. One of the Canterbury players, William Millton, of Christ's College, was destined to become New Zealand's first representative captain. The team played only three matches, losing 7–3 to Auckland Provincial Clubs and beating Nelson Clubs 12–0 and Wellington-Wairarapa 18½–1.

It was the turn of the combined Dunedin and Union clubs to make a northern tour in 1877. The clubs spent half the season preparing for the tour, with much attention being given to training. A successful fancy dress ball, held to raise funds for the trip, got more press publicity than half a dozen football games would have received. The tour was by far the most successful of the era, with games being played against Christchurch Clubs, Auckland Provincial Clubs, Nelson Clubs, Wellington Clubs, Temuka and Timaru. The tourists won five of their six encounters and drew the other. Not a point was scored against them during the tour. Their game against Taranaki was abandoned after the Dunedin captain refused to take the field because his team was too unwell after a very rough passage on the boat.

When the team arrived home they were given a hero's welcome by a large crowd, and then treated to a mayoral banquet. After six years of compromise and confusion, rugby had at last arrived in Dunedin.

The 1877 Dunedin Clubs side which toured New Zealand.
Dunedin Rugby Football Club

A typical group of early colonials. It was men like this who spread the rugby game like fire in the pig fern.
New Zealand Rugby Museum

Further new clubs were established in 1877 in Wanganui, Rangitikei, Waikato, Wairoa (Taranaki), Wellington and Canterbury (three). It was reported that an excellent club competition took place in southern Taranaki, with three teams participating. The six Auckland city clubs also continued to successfully conduct their interclub competition.

The same year, New Zealand's first rugby fatality occurred when Parnell player Frederick Pilling died after charging head-down into a Ponsonby player. Pilling's death led to agitation against the game and to accusations that rugby was too dangerous. The coroner who presided over the inquest didn't do anything for rugby's image when he said: 'The game of football is only worthy of savages.' The fledgling Hamilton club, of which Pilling had been a founder member, suspended play for the rest of 1877, 'owing to the late melancholy and fatal accident to one of the founders'.

Notwithstanding the tragedy in Auckland, rugby was steadily spreading through the country, initially in the urban areas and then progressively into rural locations. Playing surfaces in New Zealand suited rugby football, probably more than any other game, and farmers' paddocks were in steady demand. It was not an uncommon sight at the beginning of a season to see players, armed with buckets and spades, removing stones and other undesirable material from the playing area.

New clubs began springing up all over the country; by this time the local versions of hybrid football had completely disappeared. Earlier, most clubs had titled themselves 'football' clubs. With the advent of rugby, they generally referred to themselves as 'rugby football' clubs. In less than ten years, seventy-eight clubs had been established, and this was only the start of the deluge. The fire in the pig fern had begun to take hold.

From 1880 on, the number of clubs began to explode. In Dunedin, for example, there were 11 clubs in 1881 and by 1886 this had more than doubled to 24 clubs. Many of these so-called clubs were little more than a collection of enthusiastic individuals and mates who formed themselves into a team. These clubs had little formal structure or organisation, but they helped to take the game into virtually every corner of the country. They often had some weird and wonderful names, such as True Blues, Black Rose, All Saints, Native Rose, Silver Stars, Onehunga Blue Bells, Dunedin Brigands, Helensville Kauri Rickers, Tapu Jolly Boys, Star of Waltham, Choristers, Taylorville Arabs, Dunedin Chancellery, Moonlight, Thames Rough and Ready, Daisy Clippers and Petane Ferncrushers, to name a few.

While some of the names might have sounded like the very essence of virtue, their conduct and activity was not always of impeccable standard. At one club match in 1890 a team insisted on a try not allowed them by the referee and then also insisted on having a place-kick at goal. In the same game, one player made himself particularly objectionable to his opponents by his unsportsmanlike conduct in intercepting a pass. In another early club match, the two sides arranged to change ends every half-hour. At each change the players took the opportunity to imbibe some alcoholic beverage and then recommenced proceedings with increased enthusiasm.

Club rugby certainly wasn't anything like we know it today. Things were very much rough and ready. There was little regard for the fifteen-a-side

An unknown early New Zealand club team, circa 1885.

rule. Often it was a matter of splitting the number of players who had turned up into two equal sides and it was not unknown to recruit players from among the spectators at the ground. Playing areas were normally marked by sticks stuck in the ground at set intervals along the sideline, usually measured by stepping the distance out.

Few grounds had any facilities. Players generally arrived in their playing gear and went home covered in mud, wearing the same gear. The alternative was a quick change behind the bushes. Showers, even cold showers, were unheard of. The players were lucky if there was as much as a well-water hand-pump anywhere, to wash the dirt off.

Playing norms were not much better. An account of a club match in 1889 describes 'the shades of evening coming rapidly over the scene and making it impossible to distinguish the players or the position of the ball'. The game continued for about eight minutes after darkness had descended until the players were completely lost to each other's sight, before the referee called time.

At the same time as the explosion of clubs was taking place, local interclub competitions were being established at senior and junior level. Many clubs fielded teams only in the junior grade and were, in fact, regarded as junior clubs. Often the senior and junior competitions were run by different local organisations. With the formation of rugby unions during the 1880s (see Chapter 12) interclub competitions were able to be better organised. It was also not unusual for a club belonging to one district or union to play regular home and away fixtures against a club located in a neighbouring district or union. Travel to and from these matches was part of the social camaraderie of the occasion. Until this time, many early clubs had affiliated directly with the Rugby Football Union in England, but with the advent of the New Zealand provincial unions, this practice soon ceased.

Dunedin Football Club member's card, 1881.
New Zealand Rugby Museum

It was apparent that rugby had already become the favourite game in New Zealand when a significant comment appeared in the *Grey River Argus* on 24 July 1882: 'On Saturday last, the above named clubs met for the first time on the Camp Reserve to try their skill and strength in the national game of football.' Rugby had, only thirteen years after the first game, achieved the celebrated status of New Zealand's national game.

In 1885, the first and only issue of the *New Zealand Rugby Football Annual* appeared, edited by Samuel Sleigh of Dunedin. This was the first entirely New Zealand rugby book to be published, and contained contributions from each of the four major unions, as well as editorial comment, results and other information.

By 1890 rugby had come of age in New Zealand. In the first twenty-one years of rugby, the progress had been amazing. More than 700 clubs had been established. Many of these clubs did not survive for very long; some existed for just a season or two. A shifting population and a developing country were mainly responsible for their demise. Such were the development pains of the game in this country. A lot of the clubs adopted more orthodox names or amalgamated to form clubs that still survive today. Writing a century later in *The Pride of Southern Rebels*, Sean O'Hagen commented:

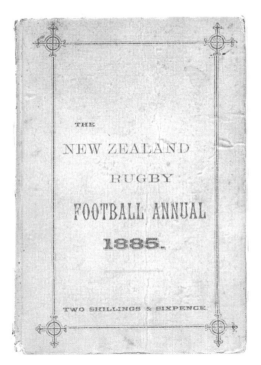

Samuel Sleigh's 1885 *New Zealand Rugby Football Annual.*
New Zealand Rugby Museum

The laws of the Rugby Football Union were everywhere, there were rugby enthusiasts arriving from the old country at odd times bringing with them new ideas, and most importantly the rugby players of the time were not drongos but men prepared to employ any extant move if it would help them win.

The arrival of more English settlers continued to give added impetus to the game, which was already flourishing. Life, however, was not without hiccups.

In 1890, the Auckland club competition had run into serious difficulties, with most of the better players gravitating to the top club, Ponsonby. Some clubs were having difficulty fielding teams, some were refusing to play Ponsonby, and, in 1891, the oldest club, the Auckland club, ceased to function, leaving only three regular senior teams in the competition.

The Auckland Rugby Union responded quickly by introducing the Districts Scheme, a copy of the scheme introduced by Sydney University some years earlier. The city was divided into seven clearly defined geographic districts: Ponsonby, City, Newton, Grafton, Parnell, North Shore and Suburbs. Players had to play for the club of the district in which they lived. There were no exceptions. All other clubs, of which there were several, were designated to play in the second- and third-grade competitions. The hastily drawn-up scheme was a winner, and the Auckland rugby competition took off in a way that it never had before.

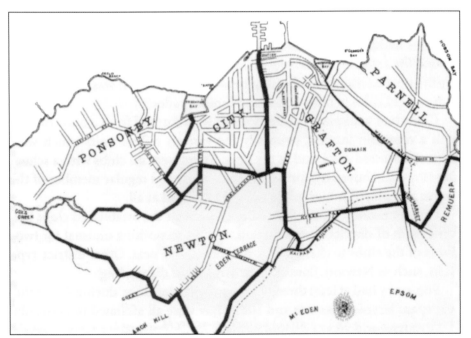

Map of the original 1891 Auckland District Scheme which saved Auckland club rugby.

Many clubs throughout the country were so-called 'free' clubs and did not affiliate with the local unions, preferring to arrange their own fixtures. This was a factor that also contributed to their demise, because players eventually gravitated to affiliated clubs that could offer them regular fixtures and possible representative team selection. Some unions also prohibited affiliated players from playing against unaffiliated players.

One of the interesting features that occurred towards the end of the period was the development of strong rivalries between leading clubs. Encounters between Ponsonby and City in Auckland, the Wellington club and Poneke in Wellington, the Christchurch club and Linwood in Christchurch, and Kaikorai and Alhambra in Dunedin, were local derbies and often the showpieces of the season.

Not all clubs played Saturday rugby. In 1895 four clubs formed the Wairarapa Thursday Union and were progressively joined by eight others until the Thursday union, a sub-union of the Wairarapa union, had more teams under its control than the parent union. A similar situation also existed in Wellington, where a regular Wednesday mercantile club competition was played. It is likely that similar mercantile competitions were played in other centres. These mid-week competitions lasted until 1908, when the Saturday half-holiday became general, and Saturday became enshrined as New Zealand's day of leisure — and rugby.

The period to 1900 was a very colourful one in the history of New Zealand grass-roots rugby. As communications and transportation improved, as player numbers increased and non-playing coaches and administrators emerged, as effective systems of administration were put in place at the local level, so order steadily overcame chaos. Playing surfaces were improving, new standardised Gilbert balls were available and the rules were generally understood. Club rugby was flourishing in town and country throughout most of New Zealand.

If a man could not good-naturedly put up with a tumble
Or if he objected to a kick across the shin.
Then perhaps he had better stay at home
and devote his energies to . . . gentle crafts

Anonymous

Of Umpires, Refs and Whistles

ONCE THE LAWS of the Game were put in place in 1871, umpires began appearing on the rugby field, the first recorded occasion being that year's England versus Scotland international, which was umpired by Rev. Hely Almond.

Umpires, it seems, generally wandered all over the pitch carrying sticks. They responded to appeals from players, in the same way as a cricket umpire responds to appeals from players. Only after an appeal was made could they respond by raising their sticks to uphold the appeal or by dipping them to refuse it. Captains still played an important part in controlling the conduct of the game.

In 1875 referees were introduced. Their role was principally to adjudicate on the decisions of umpires and captains. Gradually, the referees assumed more control of the game, the appeal system disappeared and umpires began fulfilling more of an advisory role on the field.

New Zealand referee William Atack is said to have been the first rugby referee in the world to use a whistle. Atack used a dog whistle while controlling a game in Christchurch in 1884 and some years later he commented, 'The referee had to use his voice to stop the game and when both sides were appealing, the voice had to be exercised loudly, and he found it exhausting.' He explained that one day, his fingers strayed into his waistcoat pocket, where there was a dog whistle. It occurred to him that it would be a sensible thing to use the whistle to stop the game. The next time he refereed, he called the teams together at the start of the game, and at his suggestion, they agreed to play to the whistle. It was a great success and was speedily adopted all over the country.

In 1885 the Rugby Football Union issued a circular stating that there should be one referee, who should be provided with a whistle, and two umpires, both provided with sticks. In 1892, the umpires were converted into 'touch judges', located on the sideline and carrying flags instead of sticks. In today's modern game, line umpires have to some extent re-assumed the role of advising the referee and drawing serious violations to his attention.

Inquisitive old gentleman – "Who won?" ... First football player – "We lost!"
Inquisitive old gentleman – "What have you got in that bag?"
Second football player – "The umpire!"

Early rugby cartoon. The popularity of referees has been a longstanding issue.

Chapter Eleven
The Pioneer Colleges

A Nelson College old boy wrote in the 1906 *Nelsonian*: 'If the walls had been provided with phonographs and the voices of the old masters and scholars could be heard again, it would be like listening to voices from another world.' Not only were they living in a different world at that time, but they were playing a game of rugby that was hardly recognisable when compared with the modern game. Nevertheless, they were the pioneers of secondary school rugby in New Zealand.

In the years following 1870 the *Nelson Examiner* reported various fixtures involving Nelson College players and the Nelson Rugby Football Club. Variety was often provided by mixing the teams and playing different combinations of the two teams, determined largely by who turned up. Following the 1870 game against Wellington, annual fixtures, soon to become home and away, were played each year except 1874 between the Wellington Football Club and combined Nelson clubs, with the players chosen from both the Nelson club and Nelson College. In the first outside match when Wellington visited Nelson in 1872, the Nelson club's team included four college players.

The year 1876 was a momentous one. Nelson College travelled to Wellington to play Wellington College in the first inter-secondary school rugby game in New Zealand. It was also probably the first inter-secondary school game in the world played outside Britain. The team

Nelson College. The wooden building was completed in 1861, at the time the largest building in the colony. It was destroyed by fire in 1904.

arrived at 8 a.m. on 20 July 1876, after a rough crossing on the SS *Phoebe*, and played the same day. The game, played at the Basin Reserve, was won by Wellington by two potted goals and a try, the final score being 14–0. The match was played for four spells of thirty minutes and it was almost dark when it finished.

F.M. Leckie described the game in *The Early History of Wellington College*:

At a quarter to three the game commenced, the ball being kicked off by Burnes for Wellington. Nelson having won the choice of goals, took the southern one, whereby they gained the advantage of the little wind there was at the time.

The ball, being kicked off, was immediately seized by the Nelsonians, who after a short hard tussle brought it down to the Wellington quarters, where they made Wellington, in order to save themselves, touch it down behind their goal some three or four times. Time was then called, and Wellington took the wind to their aid and made more out of it than did Nelson, for Brandon, by a splendid rush, took the ball behind the Nelson post, but, unfortunately, could not touch-down in time, and was robbed of the honour of procuring for Wellington the first touch-down, by St John, who was following up 'like a man'. The 'try' which was made by Burnes, did not succeed, though he shortly afterwards made up for it by securing for the Wellington Collegians their first goal.

Shortly after this, time was called, and Wellington again had to struggle against the balmy breeze, but to the surprise of everyone kept the ball in close proximity to the Nelson goal, Burnes' kicking at this point being most effective, and also Brandon's fine forward play. His following up and the following up of both sides was a lesson which the Wellington Club ought to take pattern by, as they are, we are sorry to say, very backward in coming forward.

At twenty-five minutes to five, the last half hour was started. Wellington again having the small advantage of the wind, which was, at this period, almost entirely gone. They soon walked the ball down to the Nelson goal and Brandon by a magnificent kick obtained another goal for Wellington.

At this point of the game, Nelson seemed to wake up, and with Firth at their head, they kept the ball close up to the Wellington goal until time was called. It was dark then and there were only five minutes to go. Thus Wellington was victorious by two goals and one try to nothing [sic], after one of the best games ever played on the Basin Reserve.

For Nelson, Vickerman, Firth and Thompson tried hard to save defeat. For Wellington, Burnes, Barton and C. Brandon being well backed up by the others, played splendidly.

It appears Nelson fielded only thirteen players to Wellington's fifteen. J.G. McKay, Nelson College historian, researched newspaper and shipping records and concluded that the Nelson team was: G.H. Harkness (captain), Joseph Firth, T.A. Askew, W. Andrew, H. Burnett, C.A. Halliday, C.W. Hodgson, P.A. McKellar, F.H. Richmond, W. Rout, F.A. Thompson, A.H. Vickerman, R.B. Roy. The school roll at this time was seventy-four. The Wellington team was: A.W.G. Burnes (captain), J. Bannister, W. Barton, C.S. Brandon, J.P. Brandon, E.F. Butts, D.G.A. Cooper, H.B. Kirk, H.J. Luxford, A. Martin, A.W. Morrah, G. St John, F. Taylor, J. Taylor, J.C. Webb.

The 1876 Nelson College team. Although this purports to be the 1876 team, it is probably an 1878 team including three outsiders. J.P. Firth at centre with ball.
Nelson College

Hubert Burnett, a member of the Nelson team, stated in a letter written several years later: 'One detail very firmly fixed in my mind is that we played two men short. We tried to get Wellington to play thirteen men only, without success. I expect they considered, that as they allowed Firth to play for us (he having very recently become a Junior Master) his 16½ stone would largely equalise the weights of the teams.'

Leckie commented on the Nelson College team:

The Nelson boys were the favourites, being a heavy lot; they also had the distinct advantage of having an able coach in Mr Firth. As the Nelson team went on to the ground their stature and uniform physique was favourably commented on, and it is doubtful whether any school will ever put into the field such teams as Nelson College did in the years 1876 and 1877, the members of which were certainly more adult than the usual college boy. Firth's height was by no means so apparent in the line-out when standing in company with Francis Richmond and others. Both these players as well as Burnett and another wore beards and side whiskers of the Dundreary type. We could only sport two boys with beards, Adam Burnes and W. Barton.

Also of interest is Leckie's comment on Adam Burnes, the Wellington captain. '. . . As a youth in his late teens he was practically a full grown man, being tall, active and powerful. He was very bald and wore a black bushy beard. This, added to the tail coat and trousers which he habitually wore, completed the picture of the "Old-un".' Burnes would have been a remarkable figure in any school, but his prowess as a player was legendary. In 1875 he had the distinction of being the first schoolboy to represent Wellington, when he played against the Auckland Provincial Clubs team.

A return match was played in Nelson on 6 September of the same year. The Nelson College team had been reorganised and had a full complement of fifteen players. Nelson won the match by 7–2. Leckie again: 'It is not quite clear . . . how Mr Firth came to be playing in these first two matches, as he was fourth master at Nelson College. He would be well on in his teens — a mountain of bone and sinew and worth any two or three ordinary boys.'

Games between Nelson College and Wellington College continued to be played in most years until 1904. Some interesting statistics are recorded on the 1878 Nelson College team that illustrate the small stature of secondary school players of the period: average age, 15½ years; average weight, 9 st 9 lb (62 kg); average height, 5 ft 6 in (168 cm). These figures should be viewed in the context of a total school roll of seventy-eight with an age spread of probably ten to eighteen years.

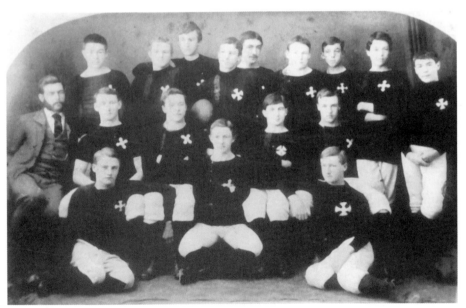

The oldest Wellington College First XV photograph, 1882. J.P. Firth on left.
Wellington College

Joseph Pentland Firth, who became one of the outstanding pioneer figures of New Zealand rugby, grew up in Cobden, near Greymouth, and arrived at Nelson College in 1873 as a pupil on a rural scholarship. He was appointed a junior master in 1875 and held that post for six years, during which time he captained various college rugby teams. He represented both Nelson and Wellington at rugby.

In 1878, while still a master at Nelson College, he accepted an invitation to referee the match between Nelson and Wellington Colleges. Carried away by the mounting excitement of the last spell, he was galvanised into action when a Wellington boy made

J.P. Firth, 'Mr Rugby'.
Wellington College

a brilliant break. This was brought to an untimely end only by a devastating tackle by the referee. On realising his mistake, Firth apologised profusely and awarded a penalty kick to Wellington. The players forgave this interference, the spectators smiled understandingly and the game proceeded in an amiable fashion. The game resulted in a 3–3 draw.

In 1881 he transferred to Wellington College for five years before becoming gymnasium master at Christ's College in 1886. Serious attempts had been made to introduce Victorian rules to Wellington College in 1879 and for a while rugby ceased to be played and Victorian rules took hold at the school. The arrival of Firth in 1881 led to a complete turnaround and again the rugby star was in the ascendancy. In 1881 Firth represented Wellington when they played New South Wales, the first overseas rugby team to visit New Zealand. After serving at Christ's College for five years, in 1892, at the age of thirty-three, Firth was appointed headmaster of Wellington College.

At each school at which he served Firth played a leading role in establishing rugby as the pre-eminent code. As a referee he awarded the first penalty try given in rugby and was involved in the submissions that resulted in the penalty try being introduced into the international rules. Wellington College historian H. Herron wrote of him: 'He enjoyed sport indeed but revered sportsmanship. It was bad form for the coach to shout at, encourage or admonish his team from the sideline, and unpardonable for a boy to question by word or gesture the decision of a referee.' The sportsman's code was paramount in Firth's attitude to the boys and the game. He aimed at the development of the complete man.

Firth was the outstanding coach and the great driving force of the early years of college rugby in New Zealand. Wherever he went the game prospered. He was a man of impressive stature and bearing. He enjoyed an awesome reputation and had a tremendous influence even from his early playing years. He was chairman of the Wellington Rugby Football Union, a New Zealand selector, a vice-president of the New Zealand Rugby Football Union, and was awarded the CMG in 1922. He was also a keen supporter of cricket, gymnastics and boxing, and officiated in each of these codes. In the 1880s he had the distinction of boxing with Jem Mace, who had once been the world pugilistic champion.

'Mr Rugby', as he was known to many, retired from Wellington College in 1920, after twenty-eight years as headmaster. To the generations of boys who attended Wellington College, he was respectfully and affectionately referred to as 'the Boss'. He died on 13 April 1931, in his seventy-third year. A memorial bronze placed on the wall of the main staircase at Wellington College bears his favourite words: 'Follow Christ the King. Live pure, Speak true, Right wrong, Follow the King. Else wherefore born.'

From the ranks of early Nelson College pupils came not only the founder of New Zealand rugby, Charles Monro, and Alfred Drew, the 'club maker', but also J.P. Firth, the dominant pioneer figure of New Zealand secondary school rugby.

In learning on the hard fought field
May this be all our pride
That to no rival shall she yield
While we stand by her side.
Then hail your Alma Mater boys . . .

Nelson College Song

Rugby Balls in New Zealand

THE FIRST BALLS used in New Zealand for hybrid football were round balls. They were apparently ordered through local merchants who obtained them from Melbourne. Charles Monro, on his return from England in 1870, brought with him four oval-shaped rugby balls. These were likely the first oval balls brought into New Zealand and were probably the famed 1851 balls manufactured by William Gilbert of Rugby town.

In 1871, Gilberts began shipping oval balls to Australia and it is likely that these balls became readily available from Melbourne soon after. The oval Gilbert ball has been used for rugby in New Zealand ever since.

Story has it that around the turn of the 20th century, rugby was played with an inflated pig's bladder at Waikaka in Eastern Southland. The games were between gold dredge workers and were played on the frozen ponds left by the dredges. Typically, the pigs' bladders lasted about a month.

iii.

S. JACOBS,
IMPORTER OF

Fancy Goods, Jewellery, &c.,

PRINCES STREET, DUNEDIN.

Whilst thanking the lovers of outdoor sports for the liberal patronage awarded me during the last twenty years, I have much pleasure in informing them that I have imported this year a First-class Assortment of

FOOTBALLS AND LININGS FOR DITTO,

Which will be sold at following Dunedin Wholesale Prices:

	s.	d
Rugby Footballs, Gilbert's Match No. 1 … …	15	0
„ „ No. 5, Best … … …	12	6
„ „ „ 4 … … …	10	6
„ „ „ 3 .. … ..	8	6
„ „ „ 2 … . …	7	6
„ „ „ 1 … … …	5	6

Linings and Knee Pads equally low. Note the address:

S. JACOBS,
GIFT DEPOT,
OPPOSITE POST OFFICE, PRINCES STREET, DUNEDIN.

S. Jacobs general merchants advertisement for Gilbert balls.
New Zealand Rugby Museum

117

Chapter Twelve
The Beginning of Order

By any comparison with modern New Zealand rugby, the condition of the game in New Zealand during the 1870s was a shambles. However, the first step towards the establishment of order had already taken place when the first rule books, produced in England through the efforts of L.G. Maton and the Rugby Football Union, began arriving in the country. Until this time, the only printed rugby rules available were the 1845 rules produced by the levee of the sixth at Rugby School. Most footballers were aware of the Rugby School game, but few had much idea of the rules and even fewer had seen a rule book. This led to a lot of confusion and a lot of on-field argument.

The introduction of referees in 1875 was of immense benefit to the game. It quickly led to a better understanding of the rules for all involved.

However, without doubt the most momentous sequence of events to occur was the establishment of the provincial unions. The first of these was the Canterbury Rugby Football Union. On 26 July 1879, after a match between South Canterbury clubs and Christchurch clubs at Timaru, on the initiative of Montague Lewin and Robert Harman, the players got together to form an association for the purpose of advancing the interests of the game. Canterbury then included South Canterbury and the inaugural clubs were Christchurch, Christ's College, Temuka, Rangiora, Timaru, Eastern, Ashburton and Southbridge.

In personal correspondence, Lewin later suggested that it was the threat from Victorian rules that prompted the formation of the Canterbury union. 'It was to prevent the establishment of the Victorian game in Canterbury and afterwards possibly New Zealand,' he wrote. South Canterbury was very strong at rugby owing to the number of Englishmen who had settled in the area and the leadership of Alfred St George Hamersley. Hence the reason for holding the meeting in Timaru, in order to seek their support, and thwart the potential invader. The newly formed union quickly moved to bar unaffiliated players from playing with affiliated players, thus effectively removing the Victorian rules threat.

Within five months, the two Wellington clubs, Wellington and Athletic, formed the Wellington union. They were later joined by the Wairarapa, Masterton and Greytown clubs. By the end of 1879, there were two provincial unions in existence, one in each island.

Otago, which then included Southland and North Otago, was next to form in 1881, and in 1883 Auckland followed, but only after some soul-searching by a number of the clubs over allegiance to the Rugby Football Union in England. In 1884, Hawke's Bay became the first union to be formed outside the four main centres. Others to be successively established were Nelson, Wairarapa, Manawatu and Southland.

The Wairarapa union seceded from the Wellington union in 1886. The following two resolutions were passed at a meeting at Carterton on 27 March 1886: 'That it is desirable in the interests of football in Wairarapa that a Wairarapa Rugby Football Union be formed at once,' and 'That this Union do join the Rugby Union of England at once.' It appears that

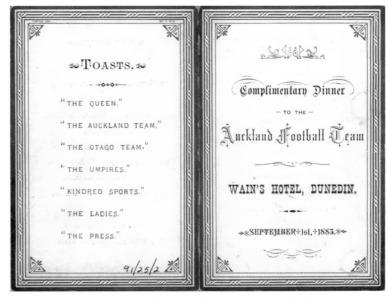

Times were getting better. The menu for the reception for the 1883 Auckland team in Dunedin.
New Zealand Rugby Museum

119

the two resolutions were the subject of a great sense of urgency. Why everything had to happen 'at once' is not clear.

The role of the provincial unions was generally to organise interclub competitions, select union representative teams and deal with matters relating to referees, the rules and discipline. As well, many sub-unions were set up just for the purpose of running local interclub competitions.

In 1885, Samuel Sleigh offered the following comment in his *New Zealand Rugby Football Annual* on the different methods of scoring adopted by the provincial unions:

> At present some Unions score by goals and tries, while others score by points. My strong opinion is that all should score by points. Who has not seen many a game where the manifest superiority lies on one side who have kept the ball three-fourths of the time in the opponents' twenty-five, and scored repeated tries.

Scoring by points was general practice in New Zealand by 1887.

By 1890 rugby was in its 21st playing year. By this time there were seventeen provincial unions in New Zealand — Canterbury, Wellington, Otago, Auckland, Hawke's Bay, Nelson, Wairarapa, Manawatu, Southland, South Canterbury, Wanganui, Marlborough, Taranaki, Buller, Bush, West Coast, Poverty Bay. There were probably as many if not more sub-unions also functioning in different parts of the country.

The provincial union system was distinctive to New Zealand, although South Africa was to develop a similar structure some years later. It was not the outcome of any great design or plan. It simply happened as a result of the demographic and social conditions of the time, and the enthusiasm of dedicated individuals. The extraordinary thing was that it worked. Whereas in England, clubs were affiliated direct to the Rugby Football Union, in New Zealand the clubs were affiliated to a provincial or district union that promoted and controlled the game at the local level. These provincial unions in turn affiliated to the national union. Although it required an extra tier of administration, it provided the foundation that enabled New Zealand to lead the world in fostering rugby's growth. At the base of the structure was still the local club.

With the advent of the provincial unions, the next obvious step was a New Zealand union. This had first been mooted at the formation of the Canterbury union in 1879, but had not been proceeded with.

Transportation was beginning to improve. The Otago team travels by stagecoach to Central Otago. Date unknown.
New Zealand Rugby Museum

One man convinced of the need for such an organisation was Ernest Hoben, who had helped organise rugby in the Bay of Plenty before becoming secretary of the Hawke's Bay union. Early in 1891 Hoben took it upon himself to travel the country — no easy matter then — and press upon the various unions his views as to why a national body should be formed. Most were persuaded, with the exception of Otago, which was happy to continue owing allegiance to the English union, on the grounds that it didn't want a group of men in Wellington, or anywhere else for that matter, deciding what was good for Otago rugby.

Hoben, satisfied that he had the necessary support, convened a preliminary meeting of provincial unions at the Club Hotel, Wellington on 7 November 1891. The meeting was taken up largely with objections from the Otago delegate, J.G. Waters, with equally lengthy replies from Hoben and other delegates. A draft constitution of twenty-six points, proposed by Hoben, raised scarcely a dissenting voice, except that of Waters, and was adopted. Oddly, when the meeting reconvened on the second day, Waters was voted into the chair and he then successfully proposed that Hoben be elected pro-tem secretary of the organisation that he (Waters) wanted nothing to do with.

The unions were called together again on 16 April 1892, for the express purpose of deciding whether to form a New Zealand union. Those present at the historic meeting were: G.J.C. Campbell (Wellington), H. Haliday (Auckland), E.D. Hoben (Hawke's Bay), W.D. Milne (Otago), T.S. Marshall (Canterbury), G. Newth (Manawatu), B. Ginders (Wairarapa) and T.S.

Ronaldson (Taranaki). Apologies, together with letters of commitment, were received from the Marlborough, Nelson, South Canterbury, and Wanganui unions, while Southland advised that it was not prepared to be involved. It soon became apparent that some vigorous lobbying had taken place since the first meeting, because Canterbury and Southland joined Otago in opposition to the proposal. It was to no avail.

At Half Time !!

The Beer that's made Dunedin Famous!

A Bottle of SPEIGHT'S

placed a goal from a difficult angle in 1·856 secs., beating all records by 2min. 40·356 secs.—a world's record.

Commercialism also begins to appear on the New Zealand rugby scene. An early Speight's programme advertisement.

On the motion of Hoben/Haliday, the proposal to establish a New Zealand Rugby Football Union was put and carried. The Canterbury and Otago delegates then withdrew and the remaining delegates resolved themselves into the first meeting of the New Zealand Rugby Football Union. At this point, ten unions, including some of those not able to attend the meeting, became members of the New Zealand Rugby Football Union, with seven provincial unions remaining unaffiliated for various reasons.

For some months after the formation of the New Zealand union, Hoben bombarded Otago, Canterbury and Southland with written pleas urging them to reconsider their positions. However, the rift seemed to widen and by the time of the first annual meeting, in 1893, the dissenting unions were entrenched. It was also clear that the patience of the other delegates was wearing thin.

There were allegations that Otago had sought to blacken the new union's name with the English union. The minutes of the annual meeting recorded: 'Failing in their efforts to coerce the rest of the colony, the opponents of this union sought by misrepresentation to injure it in England, but without success.' Incensed, the delegates, led by Tom Ellison of Wellington, passed a motion that 'no union affiliated with the New Zealand union could play any non-affiliated club or union'. This barred players from the dissenting unions from being selected in the first official New Zealand team, which toured Australia in 1893 (see Chapter 15). The three renegade unions had continued to play affiliated unions since the formation of the New Zealand union, but this was no longer permitted.

Soon chinks began to appear in the armour of the dissenting unions. On 9 June 1893, the East Christchurch Club forwarded a telegram to Ernest Hoben: 'East Christchurch Football Club wish New Zealand team every success in their Australian tour.' Two South Canterbury players were included in the touring side, which led to the Canterbury union (Christchurch clubs) being unable to play the annual fixture against South Canterbury. The acrimony increased later in the season, when the Canterbury union had a long statement published in the *Canterbury Times*, setting forth its views and taking vicious sideswipes at the New Zealand union.

It was an extraordinary statement, provoked by a deluge of critical letters to the local press, and written very much in a reactive and defensive manner. To be fair, there were local issues relating to isolation, centralisation and loss of autonomy that had some validity at the time, particularly as far as Otago and Southland were concerned. But, by and large, they were unsustainable when viewed in the context of the benefits for the whole country of a national union.

This was no longer the era of the early visionaries like Croasdaile Bowen, Richard Harman, Montague Lewin and George Thomson. There was a new breed of parochial diehards leading the dissenting unions. However, there was already strong division within their ranks, especially from disaffected players. At a meeting in Dunedin on 8 May 1893, a motion to affiliate with the New Zealand union was lost by only one vote. The meeting showed that a majority of the players in the Otago area, as opposed to administrators, favoured union with the central body.

A conference of the three southern unions held in Dunedin on 29 July 1893 reaffirmed their stance. It was a last-gasp gesture, a final act of defiance. The pains of ostracism, ineligibility for selection for national teams and public criticism were having an effect. Opposition to the New Zealand union collapsed and the next year, 1894, Canterbury and Southland applied for admission to the national union. In a final irony, Otago was admitted the following year on the motion of W.G. 'Gun' Garrard, the new Canterbury delegate, who said that he was satisfied the Otago men would be loyal and enthusiastic supporters.

And so, quietly and without too much fuss, the only schism that ever threatened the stability and unity of rugby in this country was set aside. The vision of Ernest Hoben was completely fulfilled. Rugby was now united and spoke with a common voice. More importantly, the New Zealand model of local clubs affiliating to provincial unions, which in turn affiliated to the national union, was generally in place. This was to generate further enhancements and programmes, such as representative fixtures, tours, referees' associations, schoolboy rugby and coaching programmes, all of which formed part of the overall game. In time, a broad-based range of co-supportive activities would emerge. Rugby in New Zealand would not be just a game, but a complete game system that would be the envy of most other rugby-playing countries.

It is appropriate to pause here and consider the role that transportation had on the development of rugby in New Zealand. When Charles Monro organised the first Nelson club trip to Wellington in 1870, he utilised the government steamship *Luna* and Stan Prosser's drays to get the Nelson team to their playing venue. This was typical of the transport available during the early colonial period. While individual players would arrive at their local ground on foot or horseback, or in horse-drawn gigs and traps, flat-deck drays, and drags or charabancs, both with seating, were popular for transporting whole teams short distances.

It was a remarkable coincidence that, at the same time as rugby was being established and developed, Colonial Treasurer Julius Vogel was introducing his loan-funded public works scheme, a scheme that built much of the transportation infrastructure that enabled rugby to flourish in New Zealand. It allowed Cobb and Co type stagecoaches to operate throughout large tracts of the country, providing reliable if somewhat slow and arduous transport to hinterlands like the Waikato, Central Otago and the Manawatu.

However, by far the most common form of transport throughout the colony was by sea. Coal-fired steam launches were used extensively for shorter distances, such as Auckland to North Shore, Nelson to Motueka, Wellington to Petone, across the Hokianga and around the Coromandel. Larger steamships provided the most common form of longer-distance transport along the various coastal routes.

Upper-class spectators arriving at Alexandra Park, Auckland.
New Zealand Rugby Museum

The advent of the Union Steamship Company in 1875 led to the introduction of new steamships, the *Hawea*, *Taupo* and *Manapouri*, and the provision of much more extensive and improved services. Steamship travel, however, could still be hazardous. It often required lengthy lay-bys — in order to cross harbour bars, for over-heated engine bearings to cool or for rough seas to abate. There were often delays of up to two or three days before the conditions were right to proceed.

A steamship could take a rugby team from Auckland to Wellington and the South Island, possibly with games en route against North Island teams. However, games quite often did not eventuate because stopovers were cancelled owing to time delays. Even the relatively short trip for teams travelling from Wanganui to Wellington on the SS *Huia* was often subject to delays or cancellation.

Gradually, Vogel's works programmes, although piecemeal to start with, began to have an impact. The first major railway line, from Christchurch to Invercargill, began operating in the 1880s, and many shorter lines were already operating by then. As the transportation improved, unions had more opportunities to play teams considerable distances away. Travel was still often hazardous and time-consuming, but the idea of inter-provincial rugby begun by the Auckland Provincial Clubs team in 1875 was beginning to take shape.

Internal tours, such as had been initiated by Auckland and Canterbury in the 1870s, proved to be popular and were an effective way of achieving a series of representative games over a short period. Usually the practice was for each union to tour on alternate years, with an itinerary of three or four matches. It was a system that worked well, particularly for the larger unions.

In 1894, as a result of the formation of the New Zealand union, a New Zealand Referees Association was formed. Later that year, branches of the association were formed in nine unions. The association's first conference was held in Wellington in 1896. Apart from clarification of a couple of rules, it resulted in the players' right to appeal being withdrawn and the referees being given sole charge of all matches. It was a significant step in rugby's evolution in New Zealand.

At the same time, during the late 1880s and the early 1890s, primary school and junior grade rugby were beginning to be introduced in most of the larger provincial towns. In 1897, the first North Island versus South Island match was played in Wellington. By 1900, there were twenty provincial unions affiliated with the New Zealand union and provincial representative fixtures were very much part of the rugby scene.

By the turn of the 20th century, not only was the game firmly planted, but critical areas such as administration, coaching, and refereeing were well and truly in place. Order had arrived. Many were already regarding rugby as a means of making a national statement, of showcasing something uniquely New Zealand. It was to lead to a halcyon era for the national game, a time when rugby and its adoptive home would advance together.

Good order is the foundation
Of all good things

Edmund Burke

The Silver Fern

(Tree Fern — *Cyathea dealbata*)

IN 1853, THE Royal Navy sailing ship HMS *Sparrow* called at New Plymouth. The ship stayed in New Zealand waters for the next ten years and was converted to steam. While in New Plymouth, the Royal Navy challenged the local army garrison to a rifle shooting match, which took place on the Rewarewa rifle range near New Plymouth. The army shooters picked the silver fern growing in the area and pinned the leaf on to their uniform pockets as good luck charms. They beat the Royal Navy and declared, 'The silver fern has brought us luck and we will carry on using it.' This was the first known occasion that the silver fern was worn as a sports emblem.

The first time the silver fern was used by a New Zealand sports team was in 1888, by the privately sponsored New Zealand Native rugby team that toured England and Australia. In 1893, the New Zealand Rugby Football Union adopted the silver fern as its official emblem. At a New Zealand union board meeting on 27 April 1893, it was moved by Tom Ellison and seconded by J.M. King 'that the New Zealand representative colours should be a black jersey with a silver fern'. The first national team to wear the fern was the New Zealand rugby side, captained by Ellison, which toured Australia in 1893. From this point, all New Zealand representative rugby teams, including the New Zealand Maori, wore the silver fern. Other sports soon followed and the fern eventually became the recognised national emblem worn by most New Zealand sports teams.

The fern has been used as a distinguishing badge for New Zealand military forces, particularly since the Second World War, and was used to mark the graves of New Zealand servicemen buried overseas. Although the fern is not featured on the New Zealand flag, it is on the New Zealand coat of arms.

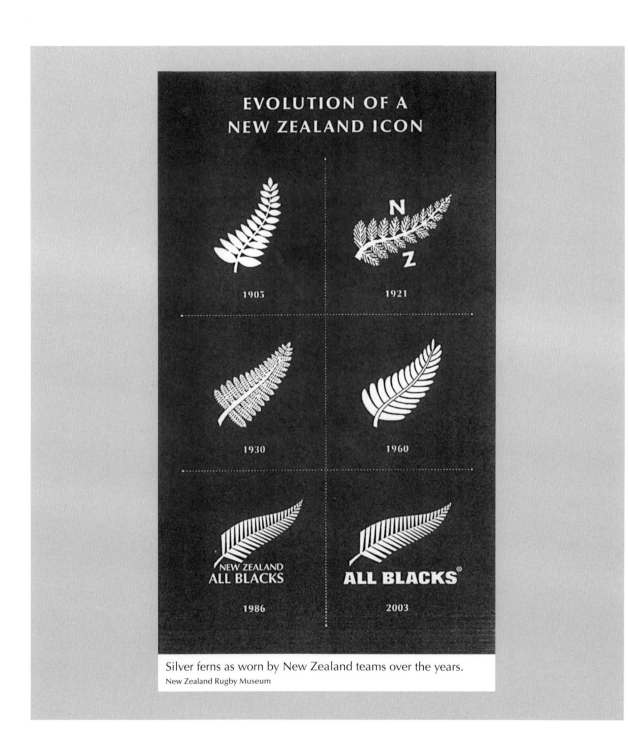

Silver ferns as worn by New Zealand teams over the years.
New Zealand Rugby Museum

Chapter Thirteen

The Game That Was, Then Wasn't

WE TAKE OUR rugby very much for granted today. Few New Zealanders will realise that, but for the dedicated efforts of a few individuals who espoused the rugby game, we could have been playing a different game altogether. From time to time, that game has been variously called 'Melbourne rules', 'Victorian rules', 'Australasian rules' and finally 'Australian football'. For the purposes of this text it is referred to as Victorian rules or Victorian football.

The origins of the game in Victoria were Gaelic and included traditional Irish activities such as hurling, football kicking, 'casting' and leaping. The Irish had immigrated in their thousands to the goldfields of Ballarat and Bendigo, along with Irish soldiers in the local military garrisons. By the 1850s they were playing a game that seemed to be a combination of many games and a general roughhouse. The hard clay playing surfaces also contributed to such practices as bouncing the ball and spectacular high leaping and catching.

In 1857 two young Victorians, Tom Wills and his cousin Henry Harrison, invented the game of Victorian football, based on the goldfields games, and drew up a set of basic rules. The first game took place on the Melbourne Cricket Ground on 7 August 1858, between Scotch College and Melbourne Grammar School. The following year, the Melbourne Football Club was formed.

Because Wills was an old Rugbeian, many rugby pundits have suggested that Victorian rules borrowed heavily from rugby. This is difficult to accept because there was little similarity between the two games. Further, Wills had earlier advised Harrison not to take up the Rugby School game because it was 'unsuitable for grown men engaged in making a living'. In particular, Wills had a strong aversion to hacking.

Victorian rules prospered in Victoria, but when the goldfields declined in the late 1850s and gold was discovered in Central Otago, there was a mass exodus to the New Zealand fields. Within five days in early 1862, 3000 goldminers travelled from Melbourne to Dunedin. Soon Otago developed a commercial relationship with Melbourne that outstripped those it held with other New Zealand centres. Victorian football became part of the invasion.

One of the reasons that prevented the earlier establishment of rugby in New Zealand was the lack of any set of recognised rules. Association football had published its rules in England in 1863, and Victorian football had produced its own comprehensive rules in 1866. Both printed

An early depiction of Victorian rules football.

codes were readily available in New Zealand, and while there were two camps — English settlers on the one hand and former Australian goldminers and military on the other — it was easy to accommodate all points of view by compromising between the two sets of rules. This gave birth to a hybrid form of football, usually a mixture of soccer and Victorian rules, varying from location to location and even from game to game. It was a compromise that most young townsmen were happy to accept in their eagerness to play football.

These hybrid versions, which included the Victorian rules content, continued on briefly in one or two locations after the beginning of rugby. Debate continued as football clubs argued about whether or not to continue with their local versions, although it was not uncommon for them to play rugby rules for a particular game, such as occurred in Dunedin when the Auckland Provincial Clubs team toured in 1875. In Dunedin in 1875, one week the Dunedin club played the Union club at Victorian rules, and the next week they played the Civil Engineers, the first half at soccer, the second half at rugby.

By 1877 the hybrid versions had gone and rugby had emerged as the dominant game throughout the country. However, Victorian football was soon to establish itself as a singular game, particularly in Dunedin, where the first Victorian rules club was established in 1879. That same year the Victorians sent over part of a team in an effort to get their game started in Canterbury. They were circumvented largely by the efforts of Montague Lewin, who related: 'We formed a union in Canterbury, one of the rules being that no affiliated club could play against an unaffiliated one — the Victorians sent out challenges, but as our rules prevented us playing them, the challenges were rejected and they had to pack up and go home without any games.' Rugby was gaining the ascendancy, particularly as more and more settlers continued to arrive from the old country.

Notwithstanding, Victorian rules enjoyed some popularity, and by 1882 there were purportedly thirty-six clubs playing the game. Rugby players disparagingly referred to it as 'the blackfellows game'. In 1893 there were forty-four clubs spread throughout New Zealand, mainly in the major centres, and that same year a national association was formed in Christchurch with sub-associations in Auckland and Wellington. The game peaked in 1901, when it is claimed the number of clubs reached 115. The highpoint of achievement occurred in 1908, when a New Zealand side participated in the Jubilee Australasian Football Carnival at Melbourne and beat New South Wales and Queensland. This placed it fourth out of the seven participating teams.

However, from the early part of the 20th century, with the growth of soccer and the advent of field hockey and rugby league in New Zealand, there were other alternatives to rugby apart from Victorian rules and the game went into steady decline. The First World War was the final nail in the coffin. Few clubs survived after the war and by 1930 the game had completely disappeared. The game that had contributed so much and, ironically, had helped to establish rugby in New Zealand, was truly the game that was, then wasn't.

The noise that was in the camp of the Philistines continued to increase.
The men of Israel arose, and shouted and pursued the Philistines —
and they plundered their tents.

The Bible

Rugby in Australia

The distinction of being the first country to play rugby football outside Britain falls to Australia. British garrison soldiers played a game said to be rugby at Sydney as early as 1829. The first regular games were played in 1864 at Sydney University, now the oldest rugby club in the world outside Britain. It was the Sydney University Club that fostered the game in Australia when it formulated 'The Districts Scheme' to encourage the formation of other clubs. Rugby remained confined to New South Wales until 1892, when it was introduced to Queensland. The first rugby union outside Britain, the Southern Union, was established in 1874.

Chapter Fourteen

The Secondary School Game

ONE COULD BE excused for thinking that secondary education was free and readily available to all in colonial New Zealand. Not so. At the time of the first inter-collegiate match, in 1876, there were only nine recognised secondary schools in the whole country. While most of them would have been established under separate acts of Parliament, they were owned and governed under various types of trust deeds and charters, and were generally responsible to their particular church or trustee organisations. Curriculums varied considerably.

Apart from those fortunate enough to gain scholarship entry to a school, secondary education was the prerogative of those who could afford it. Although primary public school education, modelled on the Nelson system of 1842, had become free and compulsory nationwide, it wasn't until the 'Free Places System', introduced under the Secondary Schools Act 1903, that secondary school education acquired similar status. This lack of schools, together with difficulties in communication and transport, inhibited the early development of secondary school rugby in New Zealand.

In addition to the first game played in Nelson in 1870, in which Nelson College took part, there were two other early games that involved secondary school teams. These are worth mentioning.

The game played between Dunedin High School and Otago University on 9 September

1871, at the Dunedin Oval, was not only the first game of rugby in Otago, but was also the second recorded game in New Zealand involving a secondary school team. The game lasted from 2.30 p.m. to 6 p.m. and was resumed the following Saturday for a further two and a half hours, the result being a one goal all draw. There were two independent umpires, and it appears that George Sale captained the University side and George Thomson, later to play a key part in developing the game at Otago Boys' High School, captained the High School team. Many years later Thomson recalled: 'The game was rugby football of a kind something like that described in *Tom Brown's Schooldays*, and totally different from the severely ruled game played today . . . No doubt it was a pleasant, free-and-easy game.'

On 9 May 1874, Auckland College and Grammar School (renamed Auckland Grammar School in 1883) became the third college in New Zealand to play rugby, when it met a team of North Shore youths at the Domain Hollow, Devonport. The North Shore team won by one touchdown to nil.

For many years pupils of pioneer secondary schools played their rugby as part of the local club activity. Often they would play with senior club players in their internal club matches, or, on the other hand, play against them for their school in competition games. This was particularly the case in Auckland, Wellington, Nelson, Christchurch and Dunedin. Often junior masters, who were completing undergraduate studies towards their university degrees, would coach and play for their college team.

At Otago Boys' High School, a unique tradition was developed by George Thomson, then rector of the school (master in charge of the boarding department). He developed the High School Rectory team. For many years, the Rectory team competed in the local competition and up until 1885 the Rectory boys could easily beat the rest of the school. The Rectory versus Rest of School match remained a keenly contested annual fixture at the school until the middle of the 20th century.

After the first inter-secondary school matches between Nelson College and Wellington College beginning in 1876, the next recorded game between secondary schools took place in 1879, between Auckland College and Grammar School and the Church of England Grammar

The Dunedin High School Rectory team 1878, with coach George Thomson.
Otago Boys' High School

School situated in Parnell. Apparently, a further game was played the following year, but the Church of England Grammar School ceased to function soon after and there are no recorded details of the games.

The next game between secondary schools occurred in 1883, when Christ's College agreed to play a match in Dunedin against Otago Boys' High School, but only after much persuasion. When the match was suggested, some at Christ's College doubted the quality of the opposition. As it happened, Christ's College won the game only by the slender margin of two points to nil. This became an annual fixture and there have been just three cancellations: one in 1918 owing to heavy snow, one in 1823 because of the influenza epidemic and another in 1944 because of wartime travel restrictions. It is now the oldest continuing inter-school rugby fixture in New Zealand.

In 1884, Waitaki Boys' High School and Timaru Boys' High School played their first match against each other. This annual fixture has never been disrupted and continues to be played to the present day. Also in 1884, Christ's College and Wellington College played their first match at Wellington.

In 1885, the newly established St Pat's College, Wellington, played the Wellington College Second XV and Wellington College had its first match against Wanganui Collegiate School.

The following year, Wellington College First XV played St Pat's College on two occasions. This is now a regular annual fixture. In 1888, St Pat's College became the first school to travel to Wanganui to play the Collegiate School.

By 1885, nine years after the first secondary school match, there were still only sixteen recognised secondary schools in the country. A comment in the Wanganui Collegiate history summed up the general situation: 'Matches in those early days were few and consisted chiefly of games played against scratch teams or against such local clubs as were then in existence.' As provincial unions were formed and junior and third-grade competitions were established, the opportunity for competitive matches for secondary schools increased. This was where the schools looked for most of their regular games. Inter-school matches were becoming a small part of the scene, but were very much special occasions. The difficulties of transport were still very real to most school teams.

1888 Christ's College First XV with J.P. Firth, centre back.
Christ's College Archives

Nowhere was this more apparent than at Te Aute College, the celebrated Maori school situated at Pukehou in southern Hawke's Bay and founded in 1854 as a mission school. Rugby was an early hit with the students, but playing opportunity was limited to the Hawke's Bay senior club championship, which Te Aute won on several occasions. Their first inter-secondary match did not occur until 1897, when they played Wanganui Collegiate. For many years this annual fixture was played at the halfway point, Palmerston North. This did not prevent Te Aute from producing many of the outstanding players of the early pioneer period, including several members of the 1888/89 New Zealand Native team.

Meanwhile, Auckland Grammar School continued its involvement and played games against teams from visiting ships at Auckland and Onehunga, as well as against the now-defunct secondary schools, Parnell Grammar School and St John's College. One of the more unusual fixtures, which continued for a few years, was against the Thames School of Mines. When the Grammar XV visited Thames in 1890, suspicions were aroused as to the bona fides of some of the players preparing to take the field for the School of Mines. The Grammar School captain, J. Drummond, challenged their standing as mining students by asking them to state the chemical formula for potassium cyanide. This type of ruse was used on more than one occasion to weed out the ring-ins. Many of the top Auckland Grammar players also played regularly for Auckland senior club sides, as did other senior secondary school players in other centres.

In 1889, J.M. Thompson, captain of Wellington College, conceived the idea of a four-way tournament consisting of two North Island colleges, Wellington College and Wanganui Collegiate, and two South Island colleges, Nelson College and Christ's College. Thompson, with his college's support, issued written invitations to the other colleges and the tournament, first held in Wellington, began in 1890. For some reason, Nelson College did not participate as intended, and there has been much speculation as to the reason for this. Nelson College was probably unable to commit itself to the protracted sea voyages when the tournament was held at Wanganui or Christchurch. Probably as a result of Nelson's inability to play, Otago Boys' High School was invited to participate in the tournament, but did so only in 1894.

J.M. Thompson of Wellington College, who initiated the quadrangular tournament.
Wellington College

137

Auckland College and Grammar School located in Symonds Street, 1879–1916.
Auckland Grammar School

Nelson College did participate in the tournament in most of the years that it was played in Wellington, although only as a guest team without participant status. When Nelson College played Wanganui Collegiate at Wellington in 1891, it was its first game against a school other than Wellington College. Annual fixtures between Nelson and Wellington continued on an intermittent home-and-away basis until 1904, when a dispute arose out of the annual gymnastics contest between the two schools. Sharp differences of opinion over the judging of the contest were expressed and the situation was exacerbated by a report that appeared in the *Nelson Evening Mail*. As a result, all sporting contacts between the two schools, which had the oldest school rugby-playing association in the country at the time, ceased forthwith.

It wasn't until 1925, three years after the retirement of Joseph Firth as headmaster of Wellington College, that the rift was healed. At the suggestion of Wellington College, Nelson College was admitted to the triangular tournament, which became the quadrangular tournament. Thompson's dream of thirty-six years previous was at last fulfilled and the quadrangular tournament between four of the six oldest schools in the country became a reality. It remains the oldest school tournament of its kind in New Zealand and probably the world.

In Auckland, a different type of secondary school competition was taking shape. The

Christ's College versus Otago Boys' High School, circa 1890. The referee in civvies is J.P. Firth, complete with referee's flag. This is the oldest 'motion' picture of rugby that the author has been able to find.
Christ's College Archives

formation of the Auckland Colleges Rugby Union in 1895 began a new era for Auckland secondary school rugby. The participating schools were Auckland Grammar, Queen's College, Prince Albert College and St John's College. They were joined the next year by King's College. The union ran domestic competitions for first- and second-grade teams. One of the early rules required that 'any player guilty of swearing or using foul language on the football ground be suspended and disqualified for the rest of the season, the statement of one of the masters of the schools of the union who heard such language used, to be sufficient evidence'.

While only Auckland Grammar and King's College of the original participating schools remain, the colleges union was a momentous step in the development of New Zealand secondary school rugby.

In other centres, secondary school teams continued playing in local grade competitions because there were insufficient schools for dedicated college competitions.

Early secondary schools in New Zealand were a little bit like early rugby clubs: some came and some went, particularly as population growth and urbanisation brought about demographic changes. After 1880, new schools that would one day make a considerable impact on secondary school rugby began to appear; notably, Christchurch Boys' High School, Southland Boys' High School, New Plymouth Boys' High School, St Patrick's College Wellington,

Timaru Boys' High School, Waitaki Boys' High School and Whangarei Boys' High School, to name a few. In addition, a few district high schools were beginning to appear.

By the turn of the century there were still only about twenty boys secondary schools of various types in the country. The Free Places System, introduced in 1903, boosted this number considerably. Secondary schools were arriving and with them the distinctive culture of secondary school rugby: the First XVs, the school hakas, the fast open play and all the hype that characterises the secondary school rugby that we know today.

Although late in flowering, secondary school rugby would make a huge contribution to the game of rugby in New Zealand. It would acquire its own traditions, its own history and would bring us lasting enjoyment.

> *Jolly rugger weather, frosty tang in the breeze*
> *Don togs together, bare arms and knees*
> *School, school for ever, on the ball till the daylight flees*

William Johnson

Rugby in France

France was the first country outside the British Empire to play rugby. The first club was formed by British residents at Le Havre in 1872, and the game gained early support in the wine-growing regions in the south of France. In 1892, with twenty clubs established, France conducted the world's first national club championship and after that there were also frequent exchange matches against English clubs. Before the turn of the century, France had begun flirting with professionalism. France played its first test match against Dave Gallaher's All Blacks in 1906.

Caps

THE 'CAPPING' TRADITION started at Rugby School in 1839 when Dowager Queen Adelaide visited the school. Crimson velvet caps, the royal colour, were worn by the boys of School House as they lined up to welcome her. She asked to see a game of football, so the School House boys, without changing from their school clothes, and still wearing their caps, played a demonstration game for her against the rest of the school.

The caps idea spread to other inter-house matches at Rugby School, with different coloured caps signifying the different houses. With all the players wearing white shirts and trousers, it helped to distinguish between friend and foe, especially when it came to hacking! Caps could be worn during games because the slow-rolling maul allowed for standing upright and there was very little running or body-tackling. Caps were awarded on merit by the captain of each house. There has never been a Rugby School team cap.

The awarding of caps spread to other English public schools and the 1925 *Boys Own Paper* shows the caps of eighty-six public schools. They were of different types — sixty with tassels and peaks, sixteen with peaks alone, ten with tassels alone. Caps were also awarded to team players by most early English clubs.

The first international caps were awarded to both teams in the England versus Scotland match in 1871. The England cap is crimson, just as were those worn by the School House boys on the day Queen Adelaide visited.

Rupert Brooke's Rugby School House cap.
Rugby School, England

In New Zealand, the rugby cap achieved instant popularity. Most early club sides, including the Nelson and Wellington sides in 1873, awarded caps, as did the early provincial club representative sides and the provincial union teams that followed them. As the separation of backs and forwards occurred, it was not unusual for the forwards to remove their caps to play, while the backs continued to wear theirs.

The 1888–89 Native team was capped, as were all New Zealand representative teams from 1884 until the practice ceased in 1946. If a player made more than one appearance for his country, the dates were sewn onto the existing cap.

1888–89 New Zealand Native team cap.
New Zealand Rugby Museum

The most popular use of caps has been in traditional all-male secondary schools, most of which continue to award First XV caps. Today, caps are awarded, not worn.

The awarding of caps has, apart from secondary schools, declined over the years, although the New Zealand union has recently begun awarding caps to current All Blacks. It is now considering whether to award caps to All Blacks for the period that they were not awarded, after 1946.

In the New Zealand Rugby Museum in Palmerston North, there is a considerable collection of rugby caps, ranging from those awarded by little-known primary schools such

1893 New Zealand Representative cap.
New Zealand Rugby Museum

as Opunake in Taranaki and Pongaroa in Wairarapa, to club caps, secondary school caps, provincial caps and All Black caps. At one stage, it seems that caps were just about as common as rugby jerseys.

A selection of the school rugby caps of the eighty-six public schools of England.
Charterhouse and Rugby are the only schools which do not award school caps.
Radley College, England

Chapter Fifteen

The First Tours

On 5 September 1882, the steamship *Rotomahana* arrived in the Bay of Islands to discharge cargo and fill her bunkers at the Russell wharf. On board was the New South Wales rugby team, the first overseas team to set foot in New Zealand and, in fact, the first rugby team to travel internationally. The players disembarked and completed their first training run on New Zealand soil at Russell. The next day, while attempting to berth at Auckland, the *Rotomahana* ran aground near Mechanics Bay. This complicated the welcoming arrangements and the team had to be ferried ashore to Auckland by the Devonport ferry launch.

It was an eventful start to the first overseas team's rugby tour of New Zealand. Attempts to initiate a New Zealand tour of New South Wales the previous year had come to naught because of lack of interest, particularly from the Canterbury and Otago unions. The New South Wales tour had subsequently been suggested and organised by Arthur Bate, secretary of the Wellington union. More than thirty players indicated their interest in the tour, but several had problems in obtaining leave. Finally, a side of eighteen was chosen, but there were three last-moment withdrawals. The final touring party comprised only sixteen players.

The first match was the following Saturday, 9 September, at the Auckland Domain, against Auckland Provincial Clubs, and was played over four half-hour spells. Auckland clubs, with a decided advantage in the forwards, won this, the first encounter against an overseas team, by 7–0. It was noted that the visitors had an unusual playing formation that was altogether wrong for the rugby game.

After the match the teams were driven in drags to town for a bath and to dress for a banquet at the Star Hotel. After a fishing trip and a visit to a thoroughbred stud at Otahuhu, the New South Welshmen departed from Onehunga for Wellington aboard the *Hawea*.

The New South Welshmen played the Wellington union side on 16 September at Newtown Park, before a crowd estimated at 5000, and, with their backs excelling, won 14–2. Newtown Park was also the venue for the next match, on 18 September, against a West Coast North Island team. The visitors won 9–2, completing a satisfactory double in Wellington.

That evening the visitors departed for Lyttelton aboard the *Manapouri*, farewelled by 600 well-wishers. In Christchurch they played Canterbury, captained by the notable William Millton, at Lancaster Park on 21 September. New South Wales won the match 7–2 and afterwards acknowledged that Canterbury was the best team they had faced so far. Two days later the visitors met Otago at Mosgiel, losing the match 0–9.

From Dunedin the team returned to Wellington. They had a particularly rough journey north from Lyttelton and arrived at Wellington at 1.30 p.m., just half an hour before the scheduled start of their return match against Wellington. The match was delayed until 3.30 p.m., though how much benefit the additional rest was is debatable. The match had been eagerly awaited and a half-holiday declared, but gale-force

New South Wales, the first overseas team to tour New Zealand in 1882.
New Zealand Rugby Museum

145

winds and the threat of rain proved a deterrent to spectators and just 700 hardy supporters turned up at Newtown Park. The visitors won a tough, see-sawing encounter, 8–0.

The team departed for their final tour match, against Auckland Provincial Clubs, aboard the *Te Anau*. For the second time on tour, the New South Welshmen were no match for Auckland, this time losing 4–18. It was later recorded that during the interval there were no fists thumped into palms, no team talks and no desperate exhortations from coaches. Instead, the two teams mixed freely and chatted to each other, while enjoying their refreshments. Such was the spirit of the times.

On 5 October, the team departed Auckland for Sydney on the *Rotorua*. The gallant band of New South Welshmen had played seven games for four wins. They had been in the country for exactly one month and had spent a large amount of that time at sea. It was an outstanding effort and a most successful first tour.

Two years later, in 1884, it was New Zealand's turn to tour New South Wales. The tour was organised by the four major unions — Auckland, Wellington, Canterbury and Otago — with all the players selected from those unions. While the team was not a truly New Zealand representative side, with no smaller unions represented in the selection, it was significant because it was the first team selected from any sports code in New Zealand to bear the mantle of 'New Zealand team', at home or overseas.

The members of this pioneering New Zealand team were: William Millton (captain), George Helmore, Bob Wilson, Edward Millton (Canterbury); Jack Taiaraoa, Henry Braddon, George Robertson, James Allen, James O'Donnell (Otago); Ned Davy, John Dumbell, Harry Roberts, Peter Webb, Hart Udy (Wellington); Darby Ryan, Joe Warbrick, Tim O'Connor, John Lecky, George Carter (Auckland). The team was drawn from twelve clubs and was managed by Samuel Sleigh, of Dunedin. The uniform was dark blue jerseys with a gold leaf fern on the left breast, white knickerbockers and black stockings. Sleigh later commented that regret had been felt that many of the country's top players, 'all rattling good men', had not been available for selection.

During the 1883–84 summer, William Millton had toured the country with the Canterbury

The first ever New Zealand team of 1884 which toured Australia. Millton (captain), centre middle row; Warbrick, centre front; and Sleigh, extreme right.
New Zealand Rugby Museum

cricket team and succeeded in selling the rugby tour idea to the other three major unions. As a result, each of the four unions nominated five players for the team, but afterwards there was some to-ing and fro-ing over selection, and several players were unable to obtain leave, so the final tour party was nineteen.

There were further incidents when Warbrick missed the steamer taking the Auckland players to Wellington and had to take a later vessel direct to Sydney, while Otago player O'Donnell was arrested on a fugitive warrant in Wellington and had to return to Invercargill for a court hearing before being cleared and allowed to proceed with the team. Notwithstanding these problems, the team made an auspicious entry into Sydney Harbour aboard the SS *Hauroto*, with a rugby ball hanging proudly under the flag on the mainmast.

The tour was one of continuous success. Opening with a match against Cumberland County, the tourists notched up a comprehensive 33–0 victory. They followed this by beating

New South Wales 11–0, and then had easy victories over Combined Suburbs and Northern Districts. In their second match against New South Wales, the New Zealanders were ruthlessly effective, winning 21–2. Straightforward victories over Western Districts and Wallaroo were followed by the third and much-anticipated clash with New South Wales. Again the New Zealanders were too strong, winning 16–0, to complete their eight-match tour unbeaten.

New Zealand scored a total of 167 points on the tour, while just seventeen were scored against them. William Millton, Joe Warbrick and Jack Taiaroa had great tours and were among the first New Zealand players to carve their names into rugby legend.

Two years later, in 1886, New South Wales sent a team of nineteen to New Zealand. One would have thought that they would have benefited and learned from the 1884 New Zealand tour. This was not the case, as the tour proved a most disastrous one for the tourists, although to be fair, several of their top players had not been available for selection. They were beaten three times by Auckland, twice by Wellington, twice by different Otago teams, twice by Canterbury and once by Hawke's Bay. Their only victories were against Nelson and Wairarapa. They played a total of twelve matches, the longest tour to date.

An early satirical rugby cartoon of the England versus Otago match, 1888.
Alexander Turnbull Library, Wellington, Making New Zealand Collection, G-1434-1/4-MNZ

The next team to visit was the 1888 British team. They were a different proposition to their Australian predecessors. This was a private tour, promoted by English cricket internationals Arthur Shaw and Arthur Shrewsbury with the approval of the Rugby Football Union. The team of twenty-two comprised mainly players from the northern counties of England and the Border districts of Scotland, and included several internationals. The Welsh and Irish were not invited.

One player, Jack Clowes of Halifax, was debarred during the tour after admitting he had accepted £15 from the team manager, Andrew Stoddart, to buy clothes for the tour. He was declared a professional, a heinous crime in those times. Ironically, it was primarily a money-making tour; most of the players were opportunists looking to cash in on their sports ability. However, on their return to England the players signed affidavits declaring they had received no payment, and that was the end of the matter.

The British played nineteen matches in New Zealand, including two against the South Island. They won thirteen, drew four and lost two. Included in their itinerary was a game of Victorian rules against seventeen Canterbury players at Lancaster Park. Midway through their New Zealand tour they broke off and travelled to Australia, where they played fifteen games, almost all under Victorian rules — hence the practice game at Lancaster Park.

Tragedy struck the visitors in Australia when their captain, Bob Seddon, drowned while sculling on the Hunter River. The captaincy for the second section of the New Zealand tour was taken over by Stoddart (who was also a distinguished cricket international), the tourists' crack centre and best player. On 28 September, shortly before leaving New Zealand, the British team played a one-day cricket match against Canterbury at Lancaster Park, and, not surprisingly, Shrewsbury and Stoddart shone with the bat.

Life aboard ship on the trans-Tasman run was not all boring. This sketch from the *New Zealand Graphic* is entitled 'Concert on board the direct mail steamer *Kaikoura*'. The *Kaikoura* brought the 1888 British team to New Zealand.
New Zealand Rugby Museum

The whole tour lasted from 28 April 1888 to 3 October 1888 and encompassed thirty-four matches played in the two countries. It was the first of the great rugby tours, and had a profound influence on New Zealand rugby, particularly because of the skill and athleticism of the visitors. Jack Clowes remained with the team throughout the tour, but did not play a game. Subsequent efforts after the tour to have him reinstated were fruitless, such was the English mind-set of the time.

In 1893 it was again the turn of New Zealand to tour Australia. This was the first tour organised under the auspices of the recently formed New Zealand Rugby Football Union. Once again it was not a truly representative New Zealand team, because players from unaffiliated unions — Canterbury, Otago and Southland — were not considered for selection. However, for the first time players from minor unions — Taranaki, Nelson, West Coast, Manawatu, Wairarapa, South Canterbury and Hawke's Bay — were included in the selection of twenty-seven players. The team was captained by the redoubtable Tom Ellison.

The New Zealanders played only ten matches including, for the first time, two against Queensland sides. They won nine of their matches, but suffered a shock 25–3 loss to New South Wales in their second encounter. They avenged this in their final match, winning 16–0.

In 1894, a New Zealand national representative team played at home for the first time. The match was the highpoint of the third New South Wales tour of New Zealand. Although the visiting team included several New Zealanders living in Australia, including the captain, Frank Surman, the New Zealand provincial teams were generally too strong for them. The visitors played twelve games for four wins and eight losses.

The Queensland state side made its first and only tour of New Zealand during the pioneer period in 1896. Although rugby was making great strides in Queensland, the state side fared no better than their New South Wales compatriots. Queensland played six matches, including a game against New Zealand at Athletic Park, and never managed a win.

The final tour during the pioneer years up to 1900 was the 1897 New Zealand tour of Australia. Ostensibly this was the first completely representative New Zealand touring team, although all but one of the twenty-one players selected were from five major unions. The visitors played ten games in Australia, winning nine, and proved to be tremendous drawcards. In their opening match, against New South Wales, at Sydney, they drew 25,000 spectators, a huge crowd for the time. Their only defeat was the second encounter against New South Wales, lost by 22–8.

New South Wales versus Auckland at Alexandra Park, 1894. One Tree Hill is in the background.

The first tours, although largely limited to exchanges between Australia and New Zealand, were of major benefit to both countries. They gave players the opportunity to strive for national selection and to play against overseas teams; opportunities not then available in other sports codes. In New Zealand they also stirred public interest and involvement in the game and created a focus for national identity and pride. They were the harbinger of great things to come — home and away tours, the All Blacks, and international test matches.

We believe in and strive to play
Thinking, running, winning, exciting rugby,
Subject to the rules of rugby,
In any possible way - - - - -
We love our game and as sportsmen
We are proud of the friendship and
goodwill it generates throughout the world.

Sydney University Rugby Club Creed

Rugby Goalposts

BEFORE THE GREAT split in 1863, posts with a crossbar, usually either of wood or rope, were used in all football games. The crossbar was seldom at the top of the posts, so most football posts were H-shaped. Once proper three-sided soccer goals were able to be easily constructed, the only H-shaped posts remaining were on rugby grounds. The question arises, when did Rugby School boys start kicking the ball over the bar, rather than under it?

There have been suggestions that Rugby schoolboys used to kick the ball under the crossbar to score goals, but when junior boys were used to completely blockade the goalmouth it became increasingly difficult to score goals. The problem was solved by allowing goals to be scored by kicking the ball over the crossbar. The posts then had to be increased in height to determine the accuracy of the kick. Today's goalposts must be at least 3.4 metres high, with the crossbar set at 3 metres from the ground. However, goalposts often stretch heavenwards for up to 20 metres, particularly at major playing venues.

Modern goalposts are usually formed by three joined sections of painted galvanised steel pipe, tapering to the top. They require a truck crane to lift them and place the base into permanent concrete sleeves set in the ground. In the off-season, the posts are removed, a steel cap is placed over the sleeve and the cavity above the cap is simply returfed.

The highest recorded goalposts in New Zealand, at Kohukohu in the Hokianga, are twenty-eight metres from ground level to the top of the posts.
New Zealand Rugby Museum

152

Chapter Sixteen

The New Zealand Native Team

IT STILL RANKS as the longest and most arduous tour ever undertaken by any rugby team of any era. Altogether they were away from New Zealand for fifteen months from June 1888 to August 1889, during which time they played ninety matches in Australia and England. Compare this with the 1939 Australian team, which arrived at Southampton right on the outbreak of the Second World War and then sailed for home without playing a single match.

The 1888 New Zealand Natives team was a private venture that followed immediately on the visit of the 1888 British team to New Zealand. Remarkably, the tour was conceived completely separately by two men who were previously unknown to each other. One, Tom Eyton, an English-born businessman living in Taranaki, had the idea while on a visit to England in 1887. On his return to New Zealand, he was astonished to learn that Joe Warbrick, a leading Auckland player and a member of the 1884 New Zealand team to New South Wales, was working independently on the same project. Eyton contacted Warbrick and the two began co-ordinating their plans for the tour, even while the British team was still in New Zealand.

A priority was raising funds. Several people were prepared to put money into the venture, including a publican from Gisborne, James Scott, who was appointed team manager. There were suggestions that the mayor of Dunedin was also a backer. Eventually Eyton and Warbrick succeeded in persuading enough well-heeled well-wishers into underwriting the venture.

The *London Illustrated News* published this pre-tour cartoon depicting 'the noble savage'.
New Zealand Rugby Museum

Warbrick, whose job as a government servant took him around New Zealand, used his position to assess and select players for the tour.

The team was originally to be called the New Zealand Maoris, and was supposed to comprise only Maori. This was to get around the provincial rugby unions' paranoia about possible professionalism among European players. However, owing to the palpable weakness in the back division, it was deemed necessary to bolster the team with some European players. The final twenty-six-man team, selected by Warbrick, consisted of six full-blooded Maori, fifteen half-castes and five Europeans who were dark enough to pass as Maori.

The team was renamed the New Zealand Native team because, it was claimed, they were all native-born New Zealanders. The truth was that one of the Europeans had been born in Australia and another in England. Warbrick was not beyond a little tribal nepotism in his selections. Five players had the surname of Warbrick and a further three had the surname of Wynyard.

The team was Joe Warbrick (captain), W. Anderson, William Elliot, Tom Ellison, Davey Gage, Charles Goldsmith, E. ('Smiler') Ihimaira, Wi Karauria, Paddy Keogh, Harry Lee, Charles Madigan, Richard Maynard, Edward ('Mac') McCausland, Wiri Nehua, Teo Rene, Davey Stewart, Dick Taiaroa, Alf Warbrick, Arthur Warbrick, Fred Warbrick, William Warbrick, Sandy Webster, George Williams, George Wynyard, Henry Wynyard, William ('Tabby') Wynyard.

They were a well-educated group, by the standards of the time. Most had attended secondary school, including six who were Te Aute College old boys. The team managers were James Scott and Tom Eyton. The team uniform was black with a crest on the chest, composed of goalposts, ball and a silver fern, together with the motto 'Play Up New Zealand'.

The 1888 New Zealand Native team.
New Zealand Rugby Museum

The Native team opened its tour in New Zealand by beating Hawke's Bay on 23 June 1888. There were eight more games in New Zealand before they crossed the Tasman and played two further matches in Melbourne. Then followed a one-month journey to England, during which the players spent their time stoking the ship's boilers and shovelling coal to keep fit. When their ship was waiting to pass through the Suez Canal, the team practised on the banks of the canal.

Upon their arrival in England, the Natives were greeted by Samuel Sleigh, formerly of Otago and by then a resident in England. Sleigh had been liaising on the team's behalf with the Rugby Football Union. Their arrival created a sensation with the public, who, expecting a team of black fellows, were quite surprised at the light colour of their skin. Also, there was not a tattoo mark among them.

One English newspaper commented: 'The spectacle of the Native Maori coming from distant parts of the earth to play an English game against English players is essentially a phenomenon of our times. It is one of our proud boasts that wherever we go, whatever lands we conquer, we establish that great national instinct of playing games . . . We gladly join in the welcome which the Rugby Union proffers them.'

The first game in England was played against Surrey at Richmond on 3 October, followed in quick succession by matches against Northhampton at Northhampton, Kent at Blackheath and Moseley at Birmingham. The schedule was so hectic that they were sometimes playing three matches a week. The Natives began their early matches by performing the haka, but gave it away when they were ridiculed by the press for being quaint and savage.

On 16 February 1889, they took on the might of England at Blackheath. There are suggestions that England agreed to play them only because none of the other three home unions, Scotland, Wales and Ireland, would play England at the time. Relations had soured after England had refused to join the new International Rugby Board that had been formed by the three unions. The international, which England won 7–0, was marred by refereeing controversy.

The referee, Rowland Hill, who was also the secretary of the Rugby Football Union, awarded England a try after the ball had been called 'dead'. The incident occurred when English player Andrew Stoddart ripped his shorts in a tackle. The English players called 'dead ball', as was the practice of the time, and the New Zealand team helped to form a ring around Stoddart while he changed his shorts. An English player then grabbed the ball and placed it over the goal line, and referee Hill promptly awarded a try. Three of the New Zealand players walked off the field in disgust. Only heated discussion between team management and senior players persuaded them to return.

The matter did not end there. The Rugby Football Union demanded a formal apology under threat to cancel the rest of the tour. When the apology arrived it was deemed unsatisfactory and Hill dictated that another be produced and signed by the match captain, 'Mac' McCausland. Six weeks later, when the team returned to London before its departure, the English union officials did not offer them any farewell. The episode left a lingering resentment and sense of injustice, which was superseded only when Bob Deans' 'try' was disallowed in the All Blacks versus Wales test at Cardiff in 1905.

The tour, including internationals against Ireland (won) and Wales (lost), continued until the end of March. The Natives' workload was hugely demanding. During March they played fourteen matches in twenty-five days. Understandably, this took its toll on the players, who were never able to have sufficient time to recover from their various sprains, twisted ankles, bruises and pulled muscles. Even the liniment that was bought by the case was of minimal assistance. The situation was exacerbated when the injury insurance company backed out of its contract.

Team selection couldn't allow the luxury of specialist positions. Forwards were pressed into action as backs and backs sometimes had to play as forwards. It was not uncommon for players to be limping when they took the field. In one game the Natives finished with only thirteen men on the field, not surprising when you consider that they started with only fourteen.

There were other adversities that the Natives had to contend with. When the team arrived to play Carlisle in the north of England, the weather conditions were atrocious. No sooner had play began than it started to hail. Three of the local players, along with Paddy Keogh, refused to return after half-time — the rest of the players battled on. The Natives backs wore overcoats and were often found huddled together trying to protect each other from gale-force winds and the hail and sleet that continued to pelt down. The Natives persevered to finally win 13–0.

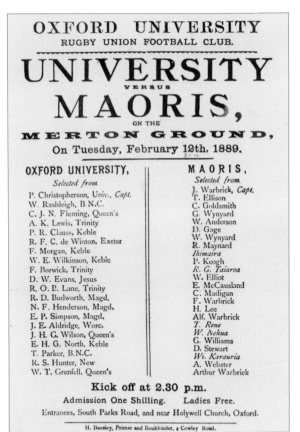

OXFORD UNIVERSITY
RUGBY UNION FOOTBALL CLUB.

UNIVERSITY
VERSUS
MAORIS,
ON THE
MERTON GROUND,
On Tuesday, February 12th, 1889.

OXFORD UNIVERSITY, *Selected from*	MAORIS, *Selected from*
P. Christopherson, Univ., *Capt.*	J. Warbrick, *Capt.*
W. Rashleigh, B.N.C.	T. Ellison
C. J. N. Fleming, Queen's	C. Goldsmith
A. K. Lewis, Trinity	G. Wynyard
P. R. Clauss, Keble	W. Anderson
R. F. C. de Winton, Exeter	D. Gage
F. Morgan, Keble	W. Wynyard
W. E. Wilkinson, Keble	R. Maynard
F. Borwick, Trinity	*Ihimaira*
D. W. Evans, Jesus	P. Keogh
R. O. P. Lane, Trinity	*R. G. Taiaroa*
R. D. Budworth, Magd.	W. Elliot
N. F. Henderson, Magd.	E. McCausland
E. P. Simpson, Magd.	C. Madigan
J. E. Aldridge, Worc.	F. Warbrick
J. H. G. Wilson, Queen's	H. Lee
E. H. G. North, Keble	Alf. Warbrick
T. Parker, B.N.C.	*T. Rene*
R. S. Hunter, New	*W. Nehua*
W. T. Grenfell, Queen's	G. Williams
	D. Stewart
	Wi. Karauria
	A. Webster
	Arthur Warbrick

Kick off at 2.30 p.m.
Admission One Shilling.   Ladies Free.
Entrances, South Parks Road, and near Holywell Church, Oxford.

H. Beesley, Printer and Bookbinder, 4 Cowley Road.

Programme for the game against Oxford University. Note use of the term 'Maoris'.
New Zealand Rugby Museum

As tourists, they were very warmly received, although at times their lack of understanding of English upper-class conventions and etiquette caused mutterings in some circles. They did not adjust easily to some social situations. At half-time during one game, white-gloved uniformed footmen took to the field carrying silver salvers, which contained champagne and hothouse grapes.

Before their game against Middlesex County, the teams were treated to a full luncheon, including wine. The result, for players unaccustomed to such indulgence, was fairly predictable. When the teams later assembled for a photograph, it was found that two members of the Native team were missing. They were soon located sleeping in a shrubbery.

Paddy Keogh, 'The Artful Dodger'.
New Zealand Rugby Museum

The tour was not without its humour: 'Pakeha' Pat Keogh once scored a try by going on the blind with the ball hidden up the back of his jersey, shouting, 'Who's got the ball?' On another occasion 'Smiler' Ihimaira, 'the lady-killer', was given a ring by a barmaid. He wrote to his grandfather: 'I have been presented with a valuable ring, by a lady of great rank. It has six diamonds set in gold and cost at least £6.'

At a time when ground entry was only threepence or sometimes nothing, the budgeting for the tour did not go as planned. Players lived from hand to mouth, always on the cheap and trying to cut costs. They travelled third-class rail and stayed in substandard accommodation that even poor blind Nell would have baulked at. They even had to play extra games to pay their board and lodgings. It was ironic that in some quarters these impoverished players were branded as professionals.

Nevertheless, the Native team, the first overseas rugby team to tour Britain, gave great impetus to rugby in that country. Regarded as something of a novelty, the New Zealanders were a unique playing success and introduced many new facets of play to the dour British game, although there was some resentment, particularly in the press, over their ability to beat the British at their own game.

Of the seventy-four matches played in Britain, the Natives won forty-nine, lost twenty and drew five. They scored 772 points to 305 against. They acquitted themselves magnificently in probably the most demanding tour ever undertaken by any sports team.

On the way home, the Natives stopped off in Australia where they played fourteen matches in New South Wales, Queensland and Victoria, winning them all. While in Victoria they played nine games of Victorian rules, winning four and losing five, as well as two games of soccer, which they lost. On return to New Zealand, they played a further eight games of rugby, winning seven and losing the last game of the tour, at Auckland on 24 August 1889.

Over the entire tour they played a total of 107 rugby matches, including seventeen in New Zealand, as well as a further eleven of either Victorian rules or soccer in Australia. It was an incredible odyssey — a remarkable performance by the standards of any age.

London Illustrated News drawing of the Native team showing the haka performed in ceremonial dress.
New Zealand Rugby Museum

Joe Warbrick, regarded by many as the greatest player of the period, was injured just before the start of the tour and never fully recovered. He played only fourteen matches in England. He was virtually a passenger, and the English never saw him at his brilliant best. Instead, it was left to the likes of Paddy Keogh, Tom Ellison and Davey Gage to demonstrate their individual brilliance.

Wi Karauria contracted tuberculosis during the tour and died shortly after his return to New Zealand. Several of his team-mates had died by the turn of the century. They had all made a significant mark on early New Zealand rugby.

Joe Warbrick, at his peak, regarded as the greatest player of his day.
New Zealand Rugby Museum

After the tour Joe Warbrick started farming in the Bay of Plenty and continued to represent Tauranga until 1894. Writing to Tom Eyton about the tour some years later, he commented: 'Teams we opposed were always fresh, played on their own grounds, had their own referee and their spectators in their favour . . . As to the management of the team . . . it was simply flawless.' Warbrick was killed tragically at Rotorua in 1903, along with three other people who were caught unawares when the powerful Waimangu geyser suddenly erupted.

Then 'ere's to you, Fuzzy-Wuzzy, an' the missis and the kid;
Our orders was to break you, an' of course we went an' did
We sloshed you with Martinis, an' it wasn't 'ardly fair;
But for all the odds agin' you, Fuzzy-Wuz, you broke the square.

Rudyard Kipling

The Haka

IN THE EARLY 1820s the paramount Maori chief, Te Rauparaha, composed the 'Ka mate, Ka mate' haka while on the run from his enemies. As his enemies approached his hiding place, he muttered the words of the incantation while his presence was concealed by the wife of the local chief, Te Wharerangi. When it was safe, Te Rauparaha emerged and performed the haka in front of his friends.

Broadly translated it means: 'Aha ha! I die, I die, I live, I live, I die, I die. I live, I live. This is the hairy man who has fetched the sun and caused it to shine again. One last step up. Then step forth into the sun. The sun that shines.'

The first New Zealand rugby team to perform 'Ka mate, Ka mate' was the New Zealand Native team on its 1888–89 tour of Britain. It is suggested that this was at the instigation of leading player, Tom Ellison. Since then, New Zealand representative rugby teams, including the All Blacks, have performed Te Rauparaha's haka when playing overseas. Te Rauparaha's version of the haka was further adopted and popularised by New Zealand military forces serving overseas, and by other sports teams representing New Zealand. The haka was not performed on home soil until recent years, when it was introduced into international rugby test matches.

Many New Zealand secondary school teams have their own dedicated school hakas, in most cases specially composed for them.

There has been considerable controversy over the haka and opposition teams have reacted to it in different ways over the years. The recently devised haka 'Kapa o Pango', which is the property of the All Black team, has added to this controversy.

The haka — an early rendition.

Chapter Seventeen

The Pioneers

THE PIONEERS OF New Zealand rugby fulfilled a unique role. Not only were they embracing a virtually unknown game, but they also assumed the responsibility for consolidating and building their chosen game. They generally had only one thing in common: they were young.

It was not a time of older, experienced administrators or seasoned coaches. These were young men still active as players, referees, coaches and administrators, often at the same time. It was not uncommon for a player to umpire the touch line for the first half of a match and then to play in the second half. Presidents of provincial unions, and even members of the New Zealand union, were often still playing club rugby. It was a young man's time and it was a young man's game.

Many of these youthful enthusiasts were expatriate Englishmen, products of English public schools, who brought playing experience of the game with them. Others were native-born New Zealanders who, among the very first Europeans born in this country, threw themselves into their adopted game with enthusiasm and energy. Collectively they were a resolute group, fired by a pioneering spirit and imbued with a passion for rugby. Most of them probably knew few people outside their own district, and had little knowledge or understanding of the bigger scene, yet they achieved great things.

We have already discussed the contributions of Charles Monro, Alfred Drew, Robert Tennent, and Joseph Firth. This narrative would not be complete without mention of some of the other outstanding pioneers who were significant contributors to rugby during this period.

To **Rev. Croasdaile Bowen** goes the distinction of being the first person to attempt to introduce rugby football into New Zealand, sometime before 1857. Unfortunately, he was unable to persuade his contemporaries at Christ's College to adopt the game. Bowen was born in Ireland in 1831 and attended Rugby School, where he participated in Bigside football. He arrived in New Zealand in December 1850, and attended Christ's College as a student in the upper department, before being ordained in 1858. A stalwart supporter of Christ's College football, he was a foundation member and vice-president of the Christchurch Football Club from 1863. After a two-year overseas sojourn he returned to Christchurch in 1877, and keenly embraced the now accepted game of rugby. Bowen died in 1890.

Croasdaile Bowen.
Christ's College Archives

Another great Canterbury stalwart was **Robert Harman**. He was born in Dublin in 1826 and attended, and played football at, Rugby School. Harman, a civil engineer, arrived in Canterbury on one of the 'First Four' ships, in 1851, and was appointed an executive officer of the Canterbury Provincial Council. He was a foundation member of the Christchurch Football Club in 1863 and was the president of the club from 1867 until his death in 1902. In 1879 he became the first president of the Canterbury Rugby Football Union, a position he held for three years, and later served in the same role for a further two years. Harman played rugby until the age of fifty and there is a well-known story of him charging through a scrum with a son on either side of him. A great sportsman, he was also a Canterbury representative cricketer and president of the Canterbury Rowing Club for many years.

Robert J. Harman.
Christchurch Football Club

Thomas Henderson.
New Zealand Rugby Museum

Alfred St G. Hamersley.
New Zealand Rugby Museum

Born in Auckland in 1849, **Thomas Henderson** must rank as the earliest native-born New Zealander to make a major contribution to the game of rugby. Henderson, a shipping company executive, was a founding member of the Auckland Football Club from its inception in 1870 and the driving force of early Auckland rugby. He organised, but did not participate in, the celebrated 1875 Auckland Provincial Clubs team tour of New Zealand, and was captain of the Auckland representative team during 1876–86. Henderson was a leading referee and a member of the Auckland Rugby Football Union management committee for eleven years and chairman in 1893. He was a New Zealand selector in 1893 and 1894, and was president of the New Zealand Rugby Football Union in 1895. Henderson died in 1924.

One of the most colourful players of the early years, **Alfred St George Hamersley** was born in England in 1848 and educated at Marlborough College. He appeared in New Zealand in 1868 at the age of nineteen, but returned to England, where he played in the first rugby international, between England and Scotland, in 1871. He continued playing for England until 1874 and was captain in 1873. Hamersley arrived back in New Zealand in 1874 and practised law in Timaru. He established rugby clubs in Timaru and Temuka so successfully that for a time South Canterbury was second only to Auckland in its number of rugby players. George Hamersley, as he liked to be known, gave great service to South Canterbury rugby as a player and administrator until he left Timaru in 1887 for Vancouver, Canada. There he amassed a personal fortune and founded Vancouver rugby. He died in England in 1929.

Without doubt the leading figure in the establishment of rugby in Otago was **George Thomson**. He was born in Calcutta, India, in 1848 and educated at Edinburgh, where he was introduced to rugby. He played rugby for the historic Blackheath Club in London. Along with his close friend, George Sale, of Rugby School, he organised the first game of rugby in Dunedin, in 1871, between Otago University and Dunedin High School. That year, Thomson and Sale established the Dunedin Football Club, which formally adopted the rugby game in 1875. For many years Thomson was a master at Dunedin High School. He coached the High School rectory team and founded the High School club. He was a distinguished scientist and writer on science, and was prominent in numerous church, community and civic organisations. He became a Member of Parliament in 1908. Thomson died in Dunedin in 1933.

George Thomson.

With a name as colourful as **Kindersley Camilo Montague Lewin**, he had to be an outstanding figure. Montague Lewin, born in India in 1852, attended Shrewsbury School in England, graduated from Cambridge University, and played rugby. He arrived in Christchurch in 1873 and three years later persuaded the Christchurch Football Club to adopt the rugby game. Lewin was the outstanding New Zealand rugby statesman of the era. His major achievement was the formation of the Canterbury Rugby Football Union in 1879, thereby preventing any major incursions onto the New Zealand scene by Victorian rules and setting the model for future rugby administration in New Zealand. Lewin was the first secretary of the Canterbury Union and at the same time played rugby for Canterbury. He was a very popular figure and often wore a monocle. In 1883 he returned to England. On his return to New Zealand he took up farming in the Methven district and served as vice-president of the Canterbury union from 1890 to 1892. Lewin, regarded by many as the father of Canterbury rugby, died in Christchurch in 1931.

Montague Lewin.
New Zealand Rugby Museum

He was one of the most gifted young men to grace the early pioneer rugby scene, yet fate had perversely conspired against him. **William Millton**, born in 1857, attended Christ's College, where he was an outstanding scholar and sportsman. In 1876, while still at college, he played in the first Canterbury provincial team that toured New Zealand. Born to lead, he captained the Canterbury team until his early death and became the first New Zealand captain after helping to organise the team that toured New South Wales in 1884. He was the first treasurer of the Canterbury Rugby Football Union in 1879, and on the departure of Montague Lewin in 1883, assumed his responsibilities as secretary and chairman of the union. Millton was a modest, genial young man of commanding presence and physique. He was a fine cricketer and represented Canterbury from 1878. During a disastrous shipwreck off Timaru in 1878, Millton plunged into the boiling, wreckage-strewn surf to save endangered lives. Tragically, he contracted typhoid fever and died at the age of twenty-nine on 22 June 1887, only two years after marrying.

William Millton.
Christ's College Archives

An outstanding pioneer figure in Otago rugby, **Samuel Sleigh** was born in England in about 1850. He toured New Zealand with the Otago clubs side in 1877 and played representative matches for Otago. Sleigh was a great committee man and organiser and served Otago rugby in many capacities, including as first secretary of the Otago union. In 1884, along with William Millton, he organised the first ever tour by a New Zealand team and was team manager. The following year Sleigh produced the *New Zealand Rugby Football Annual,* the first comprehensive publication on New Zealand rugby. He returned to England and represented Otago as the only overseas member of the Rugby Football Union from 1888 to 1891. During 1888, he completed negotiations and tour arrangements in England for the 1888–89 Native team. Sleigh died in England in 1909.

Samuel Sleigh.
New Zealand Rugby Museum

A brilliant footballer and one of the first Maori intellectuals, **Thomas Rangiwahia Ellison** left an indelible mark on New Zealand rugby. He was born in 1867 at Otakau on the Otago Peninsula and attended the famed Te Aute College. Ellison represented Wellington at rugby during 1885–88 and 1891–92. He toured with the 1888–89 Native team to England and scored 113 points, including forty-three tries, playing in three internationals. In 1893 he captained the first official New Zealand team to Australia. Ellison later became a prominent rugby referee and administrator, serving on the Wellington union's management committee for several years as well as being the Wellington provincial selector-coach. He played a leading role at the inaugural New Zealand Rugby Football Union annual meeting, in 1893, when on his motion, the silver fern, as had been worn by the Native team, was adopted as the official New Zealand playing emblem. Ellison was one of the most astute rugby tacticians of his time and developed the controversial wing-forward position that led to Wellington provincial dominance and was adopted throughout New Zealand. In 1902 he wrote *The Art of Rugby Football*, the first recognised New Zealand coaching manual. Ellison was probably the first Maori to enter the legal profession. In 1904 he was admitted to a mental hospital, where he died shortly after, many believe of brain injuries suffered on the Native tour.

Thomas Ellison.
New Zealand Rugby Museum

He may have had a greater impact on the course of New Zealand rugby than any other person involved in the game. **Ernest Denis Hoben** was born in Auckland in 1864. He became a prominent sportsman and followed a journalism career. He helped to organise rugby in the Bay of Plenty as secretary of the Tauranga club, before moving to Napier and becoming secretary of the Hawke's Bay union. The establishment of a New Zealand rugby union had been suggested several times, without any result. In 1891 Hoben toured the country at his own expense to garner support for the proposal. On 7 November 1891, he convened a meeting in Wellington at which the New Zealand Rugby Football Union constitution was drafted. The union was

Ernest Hoben.
New Zealand Rugby Museum

founded five months later and Hoben served as the first secretary from 1892 to 1895. In 1895 Hoben resigned as secretary to take up a position in Sydney. He later returned to New Zealand and became president of the Manawatu union before again shifting to Australia to become editor of the *Melbourne Herald*. He was by then a recognised figure of the Australasian press. In Melbourne he contracted a serious illness and died in 1918, on his fifty-fourth birthday.

As with William Webb Ellis, the location of Hoben's grave remained a mystery until it was discovered at Melbourne's Burwood Cemetery in 2001 by Bill Gillies, president of the Victorian Rugby Union. Gillies approached the New Zealand Rugby Union, which agreed to meet the cost of a suitable grave monument. The epitaph reads, in part: 'The man who had the vision and strength to unite the New Zealand rugby family and was the founding Secretary of the New Zealand Rugby Football Union.'

To these names could be added many other leading pioneer figures who played their part in different ways and helped to establish the game. Some of these include:

Captain J.C.R. Isherwood (Wellington), George Sale (Otago), John Arneil (Auckland), George Campbell (Wellington), Arthur Rhodes (Canterbury), Tom Eyton (Taranaki), Joe Warbrick (Auckland), Arthur Bate (Wellington), Frances Logan (Hawke's Bay), George Bayly (Taranaki), Robert Galbraith (Southland), T.S. 'Barney' Ronaldson (Taranaki/Wairarapa) and W.G. 'Gun' Garrard (Canterbury).

A curious aspect is that many of the pioneer figures of New Zealand rugby actually attended Rugby School in England. It would be interesting to speculate just how many old Rugbeians arrived in this country and contributed to the establishment of New Zealand rugby.

Let us now praise famous men, men of little showing
For their work containeth, greater than their knowing
And we all praise famous men, ancients of the college
For they taught us common sense, which is more than knowledge.

Rudyard Kipling

Sevens Rugby

SEVEN-A-SIDE WAS FIRST played at The Greenyards, Melrose, Scotland in 1883, the brainchild of local butcher Ned Haig. It was organised to raise funds for the local rugby club and proved an immediate success. More than 1600 spectators watched their local team, Melrose, beat Gala in the first final.

Thereafter, sevens tournaments became increasingly popular throughout the Scottish Borders as other town clubs organised tournaments, usually as part of their annual sports day. Along with the Melrose Sevens — traditionally played on the second Saturday in April — these tournaments have taken place in April or early May each year, apart from during the two world wars. They now attract teams from all over the world.

Sevens tournaments gradually spread to the north of England and thence to other parts of Britain, and although the growth was steady, it was not spectacular.

The first country to play sevens outside Britain was New Zealand, probably in 1889, when Scottish immigrants introduced the game to Dunedin and the sevens Charity Tournament began. This was followed by a similar tournament in Nelson in 1894. Other districts followed suit and usually played their tournaments as a finale to their club championship. Sevens had a somewhat chequered career in New Zealand, but has recently enjoyed a resurgence of interest.

Since the early 1980s, sevens has undergone a worldwide boom, particularly in countries where for various reasons the fifteens game has never taken hold. Sevens tournaments are played in such non-traditional rugby venues as Munich, Copenhagen, Jerusalem, Moscow, Anchorage, Nassau, Dubai, Memphis and Jamaica. The Hong Kong sevens proved so popular that it led to the establishment of the International Rugby Board sevens circuit.

New Zealand won the inaugural Commonwealth Games sevens title, at Kuala Lumpur in 1998, and followed that with further gold medal successes at Manchester in 2002 and Melbourne in 2006. It won the sevens World Cup in Argentina in 2001 and has won several of the annual international sevens series. Today, sevens is flourishing and there are probably as many players in the world involved in the seven-a-side game as there are in the fifteen-a-side version.

Dunedin Football Club seven-a-side team. Winners of Charity Tournament 1889.

Chapter Eighteen
From a Media Perspective

IN THE LATTER years of the 19th century, rugby was very much a recreational game based around local club matches played in towns up and down the country. The hype and fervour of the modern game had yet to evolve and media coverage was limited to the many local newspapers.

The local papers were enthusiastic and the events of the time were keenly, if not objectively or dispassionately, recorded. They provided valuable insight and commentary on the game at the time, which could give rise to some humour for the present-day reader.

The following 19th-century newspaper extracts give some insight into the difficulties and conditions associated with playing early club rugby.

First there were the grounds:

'At about 12 o'clock the team commenced play. The ground was very rough, having been ploughed for the first time last year, and the surface was covered with large stones, greatly obstructing play.' (*Southland Times*, Invercargill)

'The ground is decidedly not a fit one for football and it was miraculous how the players escaped, there being stumps and roots all over the paddock.' (*Wairarapa Daily*, Masterton)

171

'The members of the club were engaged on Saturday afternoon grubbing the rushes off the Recreation Ground.' (*Grey River Argus*, Greymouth)

Then there were the rules:

'During the interval a consultation took place between the two captains, and to the great delight of the Christchurch men, it was arranged to play the remainder of the game according to the Rugby Union rules.' (*The Press*, Christchurch)

'One loquacious gentleman who did not understand the Rugby Union rules seemed to have a code of his own he wished to introduce. It is to be hoped in a few weeks we shall have 15 or 20 players who at any rate know the rules.' (*The Thames Advertiser*)

'The usual number of disputes arose during the match and the game had to be stopped in order that a book of rules might be consulted.' (*New Zealand Herald*, Auckland)

And of course the referees:

'Someone in the County team in the heat of the moment told Mr Logan that they could not play 15 men and the referee, whereupon that gentleman walked off the ground.' (*Hawke's Bay Herald*, Napier)

'Messrs G. and E.J. Robinson officiated as umpires, but the game was in no way altered by the services of these two gentlemen, as in most cases, neither side would abide by their decisions.' (*The Marlborough Times*, Blenheim)

'Mr Jackson would doubtless make a fair umpire were he to read and study up on his rules.' (*Manawatu Standard*, Palmerston North)

As well as other influencing factors:

'The Reefton Football Club will play their first match of the season today. The match is to be played in the interval between the races and will start at 2 p.m.' (*Inangahua Herald*, Reefton)

'Budge, playing up well, only missed securing a force down for Wellington through the ball catching in the telegraph wires which ran over the field.' (*New Zealand Times*, Wellington)

There were administration difficulties:

'Geraldine — A football club was started at the beginning of the season, but after having a very doubtful existence of a few weeks, entirely collapsed.' (*Timaru Herald*)

'The senior club appears to have given its last kick as none of its members showed up at the meeting called a week ago. The No. 2 Club consequently decided that its title should be "The Riverton Football Club".' (*Western Star*, Riverton)

Balls caused a few problems:

'The ball ordered from Wellington nearly a fortnight ago by the Palmerston North Football club has not yet arrived . . . the committee borrowed one kindly lent by the Sandon Club.' (*Manawatu Times*, Palmerston North)

'Towards the end of the spell a yawning gap was discovered in the case of the ball and play had to be suspended while a needle and thread were produced and Mr Little made the necessary repairs.' (*Lyttelton Times*)

As did travel and transport:

'There was considerable excitement in town last evening on the departure of the members of the club for Katikati. Five of the members started on horseback and six in a dray and the remainder will proceed today by steamer when the goal posts and boundary flags of the club will also be forwarded.' (*Bay of Plenty Times*, Tauranga)

A popular means of early team travel, the horse-drawn dray or drag.
New Zealand Rugby Museum

'Our footballers started yesterday for Kawakawa and if they ever get there, which is doubtful, they are going to play a match.' (*New Zealand Herald*, Whangarei)

Players' attitudes sometimes left a little to be desired:

'In football matches there are some inclined to fancy play, that is to show off before spectators and not throw their energies entirely for the good of the game, but I am pleased to observe that Taranaki players now, as a rule, scorn everything that mars the prospect of victory.' (*Taranaki Herald*, New Plymouth)

'Twelve men only could be mustered to meet the enemy and three assistants had to be rung in from the human flotsam on the ground. The men who didn't turn up are asked respectfully to form a white feather brigade.' (*Coromandel County News*)

Particularly with regard to punctuality:

'It was not until fully half an hour had been lost that the captain of the Palmerston team could succeed in mustering anything like a sufficient number of his men together to commence the game.' (*Manawatu Times*)

'This afternoon there will be a game on the Western Reserve by those members of the football club who may happen to be present at the time of commencing.' (*The Southland Times*, Invercargill)

The opposition was sometimes a bit of an unknown quantity:

'On Saturday afternoon the Wairarapa Football Club mustered in full force in Mr O'Connor's paddock but we regret to say their opponents from Masterton did not put in an appearance.' (*Wairarapa Standard*, Greytown)

'Addington started with 18 men, but were brought down to the requisite number on being discovered.' (*Lyttelton Times*)

'From the beginning of the game, however, it was apparent that the Marton men were too many for their opponents.' (*Rangitikei Advocate*, Marton)

The role of women was important:

'Lovers of the rugby game delight in the knowledge that ladies are watching them, and strain every nerve and muscle to render themselves the heroes of the match they are engaged in.' (*The Press*, Christchurch)

'A number of ladies graced the scene with their presence and undoubtedly contributed much to the successful issue of the game.' (*Lyttelton Times*)

'The ground was in such a delightfully muddy state that spills were frequent and plenty of work was provided for washerwomen.' (*The Nelson Evening Mail*)

Yes, it's true. Ladies were keen spectators at early matches.
New Zealand Rugby Museum

There were occasional lapses of playing standards:

'Although the match occasionally degenerated into a rather rough and tumble affair, the casualties were not numerous. Nobody was killed and when the muster roll was called, there was no one missing, but the list of wounded reached fair limits.' (*Wanganui Chronicle*)

'Blood was drawn on both sides and at one time a free fight was threatened. Fortunately the peacefully disposed were in the majority and a truce was insisted on, after which the wounded were carried off the gory field.' (*Wairarapa Star*)

Gradually a better appreciation of the finer points of the game developed:

'Both umpires overruled the objection. The Hauraki captain thereupon withdrew his men from the field and as J. Allen prepared for the place kick, one of their number pulled down the goalposts.' (*Thames Advertiser*)

'In the first spell the ball was kicked over the fence behind the goalposts by one of the Brunner boys, another of them jumping over touched down and claimed a try. The try was allowed.' (*Grey River Argus*)

'The Yellows did all they knew and a good deal they shouldn't have known, while the Blues had to practise all the arts and wiles in the catalogue, making a very fast and warmly contested match.' (*The Colonist*, Nelson)

There was some public criticism:

'Football is becoming such a dangerous pastime that something should be done to stop it. There is nothing artistic, scientific or graceful in the game and judging from the frequency of casualties connected with it, it can hardly be said to be a healthy pursuit.' (*The New Zealander*, Wellington)

'Whenever the ball came loose the order was given to fall on it, a very unmanly thing and one likely to disgrace the noble game of football.' (*Grey River Argus*)

Progress was being made in many areas:

'The town of Ashhurst appears to be growing rapidly. One of the latest signs of civilisation is the formation of a football club.' (*Manawatu Herald*, Foxton)

'We should now like to see a general half holiday given by all the merchants and other employers of labour in Lawrence, as it is exceedingly desirable that healthy recreation should be encouraged.' (*Tuapeka Times*, Lawrence)

Despite the occasional local louts:

'It is hard lines that no property, public or private, is safe from the depredations of larrikins. One of the crossbars of the Hamilton Football Club was deliberately stolen by some miscreant on Sunday last.' (*Waikato Times*)

'Players are requested not to interfere with the pump on the well on the ground, as some careless individual last Saturday broke some portion of the piping.' (*Hastings Star*)

Finances became an important issue:

'Some delay was caused by the refusal of Mr T. Dufty to allow the game to be played unless he was paid £5, as he was the lessee of the paddock in which he grazed his cows. Mr Dufty placed himself in a warlike attitude, being armed with a large hickory stick, while Mrs Dufty stood by with her arms akimbo; but after some parley, he agreed to take thirty shillings as compensation and the game was allowed to continue.' (*The Thames Advertiser*)

'The sum of 6s 6d and a bad stamp was put into the box at the football ground on Saturday in aid of the purchase of rugby caps. The largest coin was a florin.' (*Wanganui Chronicle*)

A lot of good fun was obviously enjoyed:

'Thanks are due to the South Canterbury Football Club for the very hospitable manner in which they entertained their visitors. The southerners do not require to be taught how to treat those who may go down to have a friendly rugby game.' (*The Press*, Christchurch)

'To see the ball flying hither and thither and the players leaping after it like so many old man kangaroos, stockinged and capped in various colours, with tights and hose according to taste — expending all the various energies of manhood, was not to be despised.' (*Weekly Herald*, Wanganui)

An early club team circa 1885. Note the height of the goalposts.
New Zealand Rugby Museum

177

However, some general problems still persisted:

'The state of the ground and the ball will account for some of the miscarriages in passing and failures in kicking, but not by any means for all the mucks perpetuated on Saturday.' (*The Colonist*, Nelson)

'Porangahau beat us at football last week. I am ashamed to say any more.' (*The Bush Advocate*, Dannevirke)

Then let us all be trying, as success is gained by tries
And pluck and perseverance will reach the highest prize
So whether in the service of our country, race or queen
Let us emulate the prowess of the Kaikorai fifteen.

Kaikorai Club Verse

Rugby in South Africa

Although South Africa claims to have played rugby as early as 1862, it was, in fact, Winchester School football that was played, not rugby. The game had been introduced by former Wykehamist Canon George Ogilvy and was called 'Gogs' football after its founder's name. In 1878, the Hamilton club in Cape Town became the first club to play rugby in South Africa, followed by the Villagers club the following year. William Milton, the English international fullback who arrived in 1878, is credited with introducing rugby to South Africa. The South African Rugby Board was formed in 1889, three years before the New Zealand Rugby Football Union.

Epilogue

THE BEGINNING of the 20th century effectively signalled the end of the pioneer period of New Zealand rugby. In Churchill's words, 'It was the end of the beginning.' It had been an amazing thirty years, during which the game had not only taken root, but had grown and developed as a national institution.

Rugby was set for change as the new century progressed. Many of the leading clubs of the 19th century eventually disappeared, some after more than eighty years in existence. In my own home town, two long-standing clubs, both with a great history, clubs that I played against as a boy, have gone. The same has happened in other towns, but particularly in rural New Zealand, where rural decline and the population drift to the cities has led to the demise of many notable clubs.

Club rugby has also been adversely affected by societal changes and changes in recreational behaviour. These have all impacted on the game at club level. Senior club championships, once the great local derbies, are now often relative sideshows, with spectator interest largely centred on the elitist professional game, thanks in part to the medium of television. The game at senior club level continues to face ongoing difficulties. Similarly, sub-unions, for so long the basis of rural club rugby, have also decreased. The rural decline and ironically, greater travel mobility, have been contributing factors.

Over the last forty years the structure and character of New Zealand rugby has changed dramatically and it continues to do so. There are currently twenty-four sub-unions in New Zealand and 520 affiliated clubs nationwide.

Local age-grade rugby continues to enjoy healthy support and rugby is unquestionably still the focus of inter-secondary school sports supremacy. Travel is no longer the limiting factor that it was for secondary schools, most of which participate in either local age-grade competition, or local or regional secondary school championships which lead into the national secondary schools knock-out competition. The long-standing traditional rivalries are still strongly contested and a New Zealand secondary school team is selected each year. Secondary school rugby is alive and well.

The number of provincial unions peaked at twenty-seven, but dropped to twenty-six in 2006 with the consolidation of Nelson Bays and Marlborough into the Tasman union. Further amalgamations look likely as the professional game continues to impact on grassroots rugby. The New Zealand Rugby Union is an extensive organisation that controls and coordinates all aspects of the national game, as well as managing the considerable number of international commitments at various levels.

With over 140,000 players, in men's and women's rugby throughout the country, rugby is New Zealand's leading spectator sport and ranks as one of our leading participant sports. Each year, more written words are generated on the subject of rugby than on any other single sport. It is probably the most generally discussed subject in the country and the number one media sports topic. Provincial and national representative teams are the subjects of intense public interest and support. Leading players are popular heroes. Rugby even has its own national museum, where its artifacts and historical archives are preserved and displayed. Rugby enjoys huge status in the national psyche.

At Rugby School in England, the school and the game continues. During the early 1970s, Rugby School, like many other English public schools, faced considerable financial pressures and began admitting sixth form female students. Full co-education began in 1993 and today the school roll stands at 850, including 350 girls. Each year, Rugby School attracts over 4700 visitors, including busloads of sports tourists, who are shown around the school by senior pupils. Rugby remains the premier sport at the school, with sixteen teams active on a Saturday afternoon. Annual overseas tours by the school's First XV are a feature of the rugby programme. Most importantly, Rugby School is not forgotten; the England team continues to wear the white jerseys of Rugby School and the England caps are still the crimson caps of School House.

Other Interesting Rugby Facts

- The first rugby club outside England was Trinity College, Dublin, established in 1854 and claimed to be the second-oldest club in the world.

- No publication has done more to popularise rugby than *Tom Brown's Schooldays*, the classic English schoolboy story written by old Rugbeian Thomas Hughes in 1857.

- In 1868 a rugby club was formed in Montreal, Canada.

- When William Webb Ellis died in 1872, his estate was worth £9,000, a princely sum in those days.

- Old Rugbeian Richard Sykes introduced rugby to the United States of America in 1874. After being played by the Ivy League universities, from 1876 the game gradually evolved into gridiron (American) football.

- The first effort to standardise the number of players at fifteen-a-side was in the 1875 Oxford-Cambridge game. New Zealand followed in the same year.

- In 1882 the Otago Rugby Football Union published and distributed its own rugby annual news-sheet free through its affiliated clubs. It remained in publication until 1957.

- William Carpmael, a student at Christ's College, Finchley, shortly after Charles Monro attended, founded the famous Barbarians club in 1890. It has become the world's largest club, with international membership.

- A trial match to select a women's team for a southern tour was held in Auckland in 1891. The game was described as a farce and the idea was abandoned.

- The first annual balance sheet of the New Zealand Rugby Football Union, in 1893, showed a credit balance of £3 2s 10d after a total income of £14 12s 6d had been received.

- The New Zealand positional term 'five-eighths' was coined by a Merivale, Christchurch player, F. Childs. He reasoned that if they were positioned between the halves and the three-quarters, they must be five-eighths.

- The Northern Union (rugby league) was formed in 1895 over the issue of payment of six shillings a day broken-time pay. It took twenty-two clubs from the Rugby Football Union. By 1898 this number had risen to nearly one hundred. Within a decade, the number of Rugby Football Union clubs had declined from 481 to 214.

- The world's first purpose-built rugby ground was established in 1899, at Inverleith, Edinburgh.

- New Zealand played its first international test match, against Australia, at Sydney, in 1903. New Zealand won 22–3.

- The first international secondary school games involving New Zealand were played in 1904, when Te Aute College visited Sydney and played five games.

- The first test match on New Zealand soil was played against the 1904 Great Britain team at Wellington.

- The name 'All Blacks' first appeared in an English newspaper after New Zealand's 63–0 win against Hartlepool on the 1905–06 tour of Britain.

- The site of the famed Twickenham ground in England was purchased by the Rugby Football Union in 1907. The first match was played there in 1909.

- Rugby was played at the Olympic Games in 1900, 1908, 1924 and 1928. The United States are in theory still the reigning Olympic champions.

- The first official New Zealand Maori team toured Australia in 1910. It played nineteen games, winning twelve, drawing three and losing four.

- Dave Gallaher, captain of the 1905–06 Originals, became the first All Black to give his life in the service of his country. He died of wounds received at Passchendaele on 4 October 1917.

- From the first game in 1872, the annual Oxford versus Cambridge universities match remained the premier event on the English rugby calendar. In the 1920s, after being established at Twickenham, it led to a resurgence of interest in English rugby.

- The 1924–25 All Blacks were beaten 14–3 by Auckland in a pre-tour match before a disbelieving crowd. They went on to win their thirty tour matches and are referred to as 'The Invincibles'.

- Rugby School celebrated its centenary of rugby with a commemorative match on The Close in November 1923.

- The world's first rugby broadcast in the world was made by Allan Allardyce on 29 May 1926, from the roof of the committee building at Lancaster Park, Christchurch.

- During the late 1920s the Soper family of Athol in northern Southland made a name for themselves as a family rugby team. They all had the surname of Soper and played one-off matches against various local club teams.

- The first Bledisloe Cup rugby match between Australia and New Zealand was played at Auckland in 1931.

- The first full sports telecast to air in New Zealand, made by DNTV4, was of the second rugby test, New Zealand versus Australia, at Carisbrook in 1962.

- New Zealand won the inaugural Rugby World Cup in 1987.

- In 1996 New Zealand rugby went professional. The Super 12 and National Provincial Championship were established under the new regime.

- Village football or village mauls are still contested, often using an inflated pig's bladder, as part of annual Shrovetide festivities in several villages in England. In some villages, centuries-old bans still apply.

- In 2006 the International Rugby Board established its Hall of Fame. The two inaugural inductees were William Webb Ellis and Rugby School.

- Rugby is played in some 125 countries. There are ninety-five full members of the International Rugby Board and twenty associate members.

Monro Memorial recently erected at Nelson College
and funded by the New Zealand Rugby Foundation.

Nelson College

Bibliography

Anon, *100 Years, Auckland Rugby: Official History of the Auckland Rugby Football Union Inc.*, The Union, Auckland, 1983.

Anon, *Dictionary of New Zealand Biography*, Ministry for Culture and Heritage, Wellington, 2001.

Anon, *The Nelson College Old Boys' Register*, Nelson College Old Boys' Association, Nelson, 1909.

Anon, *The Nelson College Old Boys' Register*, Nelson College Old Boys' Association, Nelson, 1926.

Brasch, Rudolph, *How Did Sports Begin?*, Longman, Melbourne, 1971.

Brittenden, Dick, *Christchurch Football Club*, Christchurch, 1963.

Chester, Rod and McMillan, Neville, *Centenary: 100 Years of All Black Rugby*, Blandford, Poole, 1984.

Chester, Rod and McMillan, Neville, *The Encyclopedia of New Zealand Rugby*, Moa, Auckland, 1981.

Chester, Rod and McMillan, Neville, *The Visitors*, Moa, Auckland, 1990.

Collins, Tony, *Rugby's Great Split*, F. Cass, London, 1998.

Dixon, George, *The Triumphant Tour of the New Zealand Footballers*, Geddis & Blomfield, Wellington, 1906.

Elliott, Sir James, *Firth of Wellington*, Whitcombe & Tombs, Auckland, 1937.

Garrard, William, *Canterbury Rugby Football Union Jubilee, July, 1879–1929*, NZ Newspapers Ltd Printers, Christchurch, 1929.

Godwin, Terry and Rhys, Chris, *The Guinness Book of Rugby Facts & Feats*, Guinness Superlatives, Enfield, 1981.

Hamilton, Bruce, *Never a Footstep Back*, Board of Trustees, Wanganui Collegiate School, Wanganui, 2003.

Leckie, F.M., *The Early History of Wellington College, N.Z. from 1867 to 1883*, Whitcombe & Tombs, Auckland, 1934.

MacDonald, Finlay, *The Game of Our Lives*, Viking, Auckland, 1996.

McKenzie, D., *Rugby Football in Wellington and Wairarapa, 1868–1910*, New Zealand Times Co., Wellington, 1911.

Mason, Nicholas, *The Story of the World's Football Games*, Temple Smith, London, 1974.

Minogue, Peter, *Champagne Rugby*, A.H. & A.W. Reed, Wellington, 1961.

Money, Tony, *Football at Radley, 1847–2000*, Abingdon, 2002.

Neazor, Paul, *Ponsonby Rugby Club: Passion and Pride*, Celebrity Books, Auckland, 1999.

O'Hagan, Sean, *The Pride of Southern Rebels*, Pilgrims South Press, Dunedin, 1981.

Palenski, Ron, *Our National Game*, Moa, Auckland, 1992.

Ray, David, *From Webb Ellis to World Cup*, Rugby School, n.d.

Rea, Chris, *Rugby: A History of Rugby Union Football*, Hamlyn, London, 1977.

Reed, William and Swan, Arthur, *100 Years of Rugby*, Nelson Rugby Football Club, Nelson, 1970.

Reeve, Arthur, *Cradle of Rugby*, Inprint, Lower Hutt, 1992.

Ryan, Greg, *Tackling Rugby Myths*, University of Otago Press, Dunedin, 2005.

Saunders, Larry, *The Canterbury Rugby History 1879–1979*, Canterbury Rugby Football Union, Christchurch, 1979.

Slatter, Gordon, *On the Ball*, Whitcombe & Tombs, Christchurch, 1970.

Smith, Sean, *The Union Game*, BBC, London, 1999.

Swan, Arthur, *History of New Zealand Rugby Football*, A.H. & A.W. Reed, Wellington, 1948.

Titley, Uel and McWhirter, Ross, *Centenary History of the Rugby Football Union*, Rugby Football Union, Twickenham, 1970.

Trembath, Kenneth, *Ad Augusta: A Centennial History of Auckland Grammar School, 1869–1969*, Auckland Grammar School Old Boys Association, Auckland, 1969.

Other resources

Christ's College Archives, Games Committee Minute Book 1862–1863

Christ's College Archives, The Christ's College Register

Christ's College Archives, The Christ's College Sports Register

Luxford, Bob, Personal Papers, New Zealand Rugby Museum

McKay, J.G., Personal Papers, Nelson College Archives

McKenzie, Will, Personal Papers, New Zealand Rugby Museum

New Zealand Rugby Museum, Various Papers and Extracts

Ray, David, Personal Papers, Rugby School, England

Sinclair, John, Rugby Museum Newsletters, New Zealand Rugby Museum

www.gilbertrugby.com

www.irb.com

www.rfu.com

www.rugbyfootballhistory.com

Index